HOW TO TRACE YOUR
IRISH
ANCESTORS

HOW TO TRACE YOUR
IRISH
ANCESTORS

An essential guide to researching
and documenting the family histories
of Ireland's people

929. 1

—— IAN ——
MAXWELL

For Valerie, thank you for all your help and support.

Published by How To Books Ltd,
Spring Hill House, Spring Hill Road,
Begbroke, Oxford OX5 1RX, United Kingdom
Tel: (01865) 375794. Fax: (01865) 379162
info@howtobooks.co.uk
www.howtobooks.co.uk

How To Books greatly reduce the carbon footprint of their books
by sourcing their typesetting and printing in the UK.

British Library Cataloguing in Publication Data
A catalogue record for this book is available from the British Library

ISBN 978 1 84528 234 9

Cover design by Baseline Arts Ltd, Oxford
Produced for How-To Books by Deer Park Productions, Tavistock
Typeset by Kestrel Data, Exeter
Printed and bound by Cromwell Press, Trowbridge, Wiltshire

NOTE: The material contained in this book is set out in good
faith for general guidance and no liability can be accepted
for loss or expense incurred as a result of relying in particular
circumstances on statements made in the book. Laws and
regulations are complex and liable to change, and readers should
check the current position with the relevant authorities before
making personal arrangements.

Contents

We are the children of many sires, and every drop of
blood in us in its turn . . . betrays its ancestor.

Ralph Waldo Emerson

Abbreviations

AA	Armagh Ancestry
GO	Genealogical Office
LC	Local Custody
LDS	Latter-Day Saints
NAI	National Archives of Ireland
NLI	National Library of Ireland
NUI	National University of Ireland
PRONI	Public Record Office of Northern Ireland
RIA	Royal Irish Academy
RCB	Representative Church Body
TNA	The National Archives, London
UHF	Ulster Historical Foundation

Introduction

THERE ARE MANY REASONS why people set out to trace their family tree. For some, the reason may be curiosity sparked by stories handed down through the generations. Others may be inspired by old photographs, letters, or genealogical lists carefully grafted into an old family Bible. They may come from close-knit families with a strong sense of their identity, or from broken or scattered families who know next to nothing about their lineage. For many, genealogy as a hobby offers a chance to indulge their love of history in a very personal way. Others see it as a chance to learn more about themselves: from whom did they inherit their red hair or prominent nose; their love for music; their sporting or artistic skills?

Some hope that an ancestor was famous, others settle for notorious. A few hope for royal connections. Most of us have to settle for ancestors with more humble occupations, such as labourers or weavers, factory workers or shopkeepers. One should remember, however, that even the most humble of ancestors have a record of which they can be proud – all of them reached adulthood and produced descendants who did the same. None of them was crushed by a woolly mammoth or felled by an enemy spear, at least before they produced children. Many millions of their contemporaries were not so successful!

Whatever the original impulse, once hooked the family historian will become increasingly hungry for new information as his or her family tree grows. It arouses the detective instinct within all of us as well as the passion of the collector to complete the set. Today more than 84,000 overseas visitors come to Ireland each year in order to research their family history: by 2001 the Irish Tourist Board, *Bord Failte*, had estimated that roots tourism was worth £34 million to the Irish economy and numbers continue to grow as the Internet attracts thousands of new family history enthusiasts to their ancestral homeland.

What is genealogy?

Genealogy is defined by the *Oxford English Dictionary* as 'a line of descent traced continuously from an ancestor' and 'the study of lines of descent'. Tracing ancestors is about so much more than just a list of names and dates on a chart however. It should involve an understanding of history, both national and local, through which our ancestors lived. As Sir Robert E. Matheson, author of the *Special Report on Surnames in Ireland*, pointed out more than a century ago, the story of individual families and the development of the nation as a whole provide important clues to the character of its people:

> . . . *the history of our country lies enshrined in its Surnames; and on our shop fronts and in our graveyards may be found side by side the names of the descendants of the Milesian Prince, of the Scandinavian Viking, and of the Norman Knight.*

The origin of modern genealogy is closely linked with the proof of succession to lands and titles and was therefore the preserve of the ruling classes in the sixteenth and seventeenth centuries. They were not above massaging the truth to make their lineage more distinguished than it really was – something no self-respecting family historian would dream of doing today! There is a certain irony in the fact that since the position of the aristocracy went into decline during the second half of the nineteenth century, the interest in genealogy has increased rather than vanished. This is because we have retained our ancestors' interest in our own and others' kinships and origins despite the increasing rootlessness of modern life.

In the ancient past it was thought a normal part of all children's education to teach them to recite their ancestors for several generations. This is particularly true of Irish chiefs and kings, whose genealogy was passed down by word of mouth, forming the backbone of the oldest historical traditions in Ireland. The general consciousness of kinship and descent in Ireland was therefore very strong. The Irish pride in their pedigree was remarked on by numerous writers over the centuries; Englishman John Loveday, in his

Irish tour of 1732, recalled that even among the peasantry:

So great is ye pride of these common people that if a woman be ye same name as some noble family she'll retain it in marriage unless her husband has as distinguished a name.

More than fifty years ago, the County Down-born author of the Narnia books, C.S. Lewis, wrote:

Human beings look separate because you see them walking about separately. But then we are so made that we can see only the present moment. If we could see the past, then of course it would look different. For there was a time when every man was part of his mother, and (earlier still) part of his father as well: and when they were part of his grandparents. If you could see humanity spread out in time, as God sees it, it would not look like a lot of separate things dotted about. It would look like one single growing thing – rather like a very complicated tree. Every individual would appear connected with every other.

The family historian is obsessed about making those connections and this book aims to help both the beginner and the more experienced researcher in their quest. Unlike Britain, which has very extensive civil and census records, Irish ancestral research is hampered by the destruction of so many of the major record collections. Researchers must therefore make greater use of church records, school registers and land and valuation records than their counterparts in England, Scotland or Wales. Nevertheless, with diligence the family historian in Ireland should be able to trace their roots to the beginning of the nineteenth century – and a lucky few may be able to trace a line further than the early seventeenth century.

Where to Begin

Start at the beginning

ONCE YOU HAVE BEEN BITTEN by the need to trace your family tree, it is very tempting to rush to the nearest archival institution and to be put off immediately by the daunting amount of information available. It is therefore best to begin your research at home. Searching through old records, although often rewarding, is apt to be perplexing and frustrating. Even the most experienced researcher can take a wrong turn and end up spending valuable time ploughing through records that lead to a dead-end. Start with yourself, work through your parents to your grandparents and take each generation as you find it.

To make more productive use of your time, it is essential to gather as much information as possible from old family Bibles, legal documents (such as wills or leases), and inscriptions from family gravestones. This can help to pinpoint exactly where your family lived at a particular time and provide vital clues to add to names that family historians are often disappointed to find are all too popular in Ireland.

It is also essential to talk to relatives, especially those from an older generation whose memories, however inaccurate, may point you in the right direction. Conversations or correspondence can lead you to other, more distant relatives or friends of the family, of whose existence you were previously unaware. If you are lucky you may find someone who has taken an interest in the family history, perhaps has even made a start on a family tree. They may be able to tell you if there were certain occupations or trades associated with the family, or which schools and churches they attended, perhaps where they were buried. You may find out that the family are associated with a particular town or townland, and that a particular first name has been passed down through the generations. Ask them if anyone has served in the armed forces or if relatives have emigrated. If you are very lucky they may have in their possession old letters, diaries, wills or birth certificates that will save you time and money.

What do I need to know?

To make best use of the records it is essential to know where your ancestors lived in Ireland. Linking your ancestor to a county is a great help, but what you really need to do is to identify the parish or townland of origin. The county-based heritage centres in Ireland can help. Established as part of the Irish Genealogical Project, which aims to create a comprehensive genealogical database for the entire island of Ireland, each centre indexes and computerizes records of a particular county, or in some cases two counties. Staff will search their databases for a fee. If you know only the name of the county your ancestor came from, one of these centres may be the best way of finding a more specific place of origin.

How far back can I go?

This depends on the information available and how much effort you put into your research. Irish ancestral research is hampered by the fact that many records were lost when the Public Record Office in Dublin was destroyed by fire in 1922. In England and Wales, where national registration dates back to 1837 and census returns are available from 1841, it is relatively easy to trace your roots back to the early nineteenth century. In Ireland civil registration did not begin to 1864 and census returns from 1821 to 1851 were destroyed in the Public Record Office in 1922 while those from 1861 to 1891 were pulped by government order during the First World War. The family historian is therefore forced to make much more extensive use of church records, school registers and the records of the big estates which once dominated the country. This is, of course, more time consuming. Nevertheless, with diligence the family historian in Ireland should be able to trace their roots to the beginning of the nineteenth century. It is very rare, though not impossible, for anyone to be able to trace a line further than the early seventeenth century.

A walk round a graveyard

A walk around a graveyard can often save wading through endless pages of a church register for the birth or death dates of a particular ancestor. In Ireland the practice of erecting a headstone to mark the last resting-place of a relative dates in most areas from the seventeenth century. However, such memorials erected before the seventeenth century tended to be made of wood and so have not survived.

If a parish register records the burial of your ancestor in the churchyard, any headstone, if it survives, should be in that churchyard. A death certificate does not indicate the place or date of burial, but your relatives may hold memorial or funeral cards. You should also ask relatives about the location of family graves. Because so many headstones are illegible it is worth checking at your local library to find out if the gravestones in a particular cemetery have been transcribed and published.

If you know where your ancestor lived it is worth paying a visit to the local graveyard as a headstone may provide important information such as names and dates of births and deaths, and this will make it easier to search through old records. Other valuable information can include the deceased's occupation or place of origin and even the names of husbands, wives or children. A headstone may reveal the married names of daughters or sisters of your ancestors and may record two, three or more generations of a family. The style of the headstone also can give a clue to the economic circumstances of the family at a particular period in history. You should treat the information on a headstone (especially ages) with some care. A memorial may refer to two or more people and it may have been placed there on the death of the last person, perhaps many years after the death of the first person buried in the plot.

Visit a LDS Family History Centre

The pre-eminent source of genealogical information is the Family History Library of the Church of Jesus Christ of Latter-Day Saints (the Mormons). There is an online catalogue of this immense library, and there are Family History Centres which are in effect branches of this library in many towns and cities throughout the British Isles, and indeed the world, where microfilm copies of most of the library's holdings can be viewed. In Ireland, centres are located in Dublin, Cork, Limerick, Belfast, Londonderry and Coleraine (see p. 182 for addresses).

One particularly important information source that has been produced by the Family History Library is the International Genealogical Index (or IGI), now available online at the LDS Family Search site at www.familysearch.org/. This contains millions of entries, mainly of baptisms and marriages, many of them taken from parish registers as part of an organized program of transcription. Individual researchers have provided other entries, so you should always check the original sources of the information contained in the index.

Visiting the archives

When you have carried out your preliminary work a visit to one of the major archival institutions is a must. You can always ask one of the Family History Centres or a local professional genealogist to carry out some initial research. This can be particularly useful if your time is limited. Archival institutions can be intimidating places to the inexperienced family historian but you'll soon learn the ropes and in no time at all it will seem no more challenging than a trip to your local library. Details of the kinds of record you can expect to find will be given on the institution's website and will include:

◆ census returns;

◆ wills and probate records;

◆ school records;

◆ electoral registers;

◆ church records;

◆ street directories;

◆ valuation and taxation records;

◆ estate papers and personal collections.

A list of the main archival institutions is provided in the 'Useful Research Resources' section at the end of this book (p. 173) with details of their holdings and contact numbers. It is advisable to write in advance to find out opening times and details of any local bank holidays, particularly if you have a long way to travel.

You should also leave plenty of time for your research. Family history is a time-consuming business – a real labour of love. Information in old records often conflicts with family tradition and facts need to be rechecked against the available evidence. It also takes time to understand how a major archival institution works: finding documents, ordering them out and reading sometimes illegible handwriting can take longer than you imagine. I well remember one earnest tourist coming into the Public Record Office of Northern Ireland and addressing a bewildered staff member with the words: 'Quick! I have a taxi waiting to take me to the airport. Could you please give me my family tree and I'll be on my way!' Sadly that's not the way it works. Unless you are very lucky and someone has already done some of the work for you, tracing ancestors can take years. On the other hand, uncovering the tangled web of our family tree is an endless fascinating business – why leave it to someone else to have all the fun!

Document your findings

For most of our ancestors, church records will provide important evidence of their progress through life including baptism, marriage, the birth of children, and ultimately death. School records, leases and rentals from estates, government records such as valuation and taxation records, census and testamentary records can augment these. Be methodical and carefully document your findings. Avoid odd scraps of paper and never depend on your memory however prodigious it may be. You may need to refer back to some piece of research which did not seem promising at the time. If you find some valuable information in a reference book, make sure you keep a record detailed enough to help you relocate it some years later. This is especially important if you plan to publish your research. As a research officer in the Public Record Office of Northern Ireland, I was frequently shown a copy of a document by a researcher who had forgotten to take a note of the collection from which it had originally come. Their last hope was that someone would recognize it; otherwise they could only hope that they would stumble on it again amongst the more than 53 kilometres of records held by the office – an almost impossible task!

There are countless ways to record the results of your research and many computer packages exist to make the finished product look professional and visually pleasing – the rolled-up bit of paper is a thing of the past. Family historians can now produce electronic photograph albums, printed customized reports, lists and indexes to a very professional standard.

A note about Irish surnames

It is the existence of hereditary surnames that makes it possible to trace the history of even the most humble of families. However, it is important to remember that surnames have varied significantly over the centuries, and were affected by local dialect, pronunciation and inconsistency in spelling until well into the nineteenth century.

In many cases English and Irish names were used interchangeably. In 1900, the Registrar of Murragh District, Co. Cork, noted the synonymous use of 'Hurley' and 'Commane' in his district, remarking that '"Common" is the Gaelic for "Hurley"', and is a 'stick with a curved boss to play goal with'. The Registrar of Cappoquin District reported that a man named 'Bywater' registered his deceased brother as Michael Sruffaun: 'On being interrogated as to the difference in the surnames, he said that he was always known by the name Bywater, but his brother by the name Sruffaun. Sruffaun is a local form of *sruthan*, an Irish word for a little stream.'

Surnames often changed spelling according to the most popular form in a particular location. Therefore, someone with the surname Cairns may find the name spelt Kearns or even Kearney outside Ulster. In spite of these variations people with these names may well be members of the same family. At the same time rare surnames were often absorbed by better known ones of somewhat similar sound, e.g. Sullahan changed to Sullivan. It is important therefore not to become too pedantic about the spelling of a particular surname and to be prepared to accept any variations adopted by our ancestors.

Those wishing to find out more about the origin and location of surnames should consult the following:

◆ Bell, Robert *The Book of Ulster Surnames* (Belfast, 1989)

◆ Black, George F. *The Surnames of Scotland: Their Origin, Meaning and History* (New York, 1962)

◆ de Breffny, Brian *Irish Family Names, Arms, Origins and Locations* (Dublin, 1982)

◆ Greehan, Ida *Irish Family Names, Highlights of 50 Family Histories* (London, 1973)

◆ MacLysaght, Eward *Irish Families* (3rd edn, Dublin, 1972)

◆ MacLysaght, Eward *More Irish Families* (Dublin, 1960) *Supplement to Irish Families* (Dublin, 1964)

◆ MacLysaght, Eward *The Surnames of Ireland* (3rd edn, Dublin, 1978)

◆ Matheson, Robert E. *Special Report on Surnames in Ireland* (Dublin, 1894)

◆ Morgan T.J. and Prys Morgan *Welsh Surnames* (Cardiff, 1985)

◆ O'Laughlin, M. *The Master Book of Irish Surnames* (1988)

◆ Quinn, Sean E. *Surnames in Ireland* (2000)

◆ Reaney, P.H. *A Dictionary of British Surnames* (London, 1958)

Also of interest is *Grenham's Irish Surnames*, produced in 2002. This CD-ROM provides an unparalleled resource for anyone interested in Irish surnames. It includes details of 26,756 Irish surnames and 104,058 surname variants, an extensive bibliography of Irish family history, Ireland-wide parish maps, details of the records of 3782 churches and congregations throughout Ireland, comprising 8376 sets of records.

2 Administrative Divisions

I N ORDER TO UNDERSTAND more fully the way in which Irish records were compiled, it is important that the family historian knows something of the administrative divisions in Ireland. Ireland and its counties are subdivided in a unique way: counties into baronies; baronies into parishes; and parishes into townlands. Central and local government, the Church and landed aristocracy all divided their records into counties, parishes, baronies and townlands and maps were drawn up accordingly. Irish archival institutions have taken the same approach when cataloguing their records. Therefore if you can associate an ancestor with, for example, a particular townland you will have immediate access to a wide range of records at any of the major archival institutions in both Dublin and Belfast.

General Alphabetical Index to the Townlands and Towns, Parishes and Baronies of Ireland

One you have located the particular townland in which your ancestor lived, you should consult the *General Alphabetical Index to the Townlands and Towns, Parishes and Baronies of Ireland*, which is an essential reference tool for researchers interested in locating the various administrative divisions into which their particular townland falls. These indexes were published along with the census returns, 1851–1901, and list all baronies, civil parishes, district electoral divisions, poor law unions, towns, villages and townlands that existed at the time. They are available on the Search Room shelves at both PRONI and the NAI. It is also possible to search the *Alphabetical Index* online at the Irish Ancestors website at www.ireland.com/ancestor/placenames/. From here you can search more than 65,000 entries, in the 1851 Index, including street listings from Dublin, Cork and Belfast cities.

The townland

The townland is a unique feature of the Irish landscape and is one of the most ancient divisions in the country. The origins of the townland remain obscure but many date from the ancient clan lands that predate the county or parish. Others owe their origins to the Anglo-Norman manor, to divisions of land created during the Plantation, and during the nineteenth century, to the Ordnance Survey.

From the seventeenth century onwards land was let by landlords on a townland basis and townland names were recorded in a variety of documentation concerning land. Estate rentals were organized by townlands, as were surveys such as the tithe applotment books. It was the smallest division and it was used as a basis of the census returns from 1821 and for the first official valuation of Ireland in the 1830s. Once the townland is known, the *General Alphabetical Index to the Townlands and Towns, Parishes and Baronies of Ireland* will give its exact location, citing a map reference, the size of the townland in acres, the county, barony and parish within which it is located, and the relevant poor law union.

Unofficial place names

Even the most experienced researcher can be confused by references to place names in old documents which do not correspond with any local townland. These are usually old Gaelic names for subdivisions of land which ceased to be used in official documents after standardized names were given to each townland during the Ordnance Survey mapping of Ireland in the 1830s.

The county

The county as a territorial division dates from the Norman conquest of Ireland during the twelfth century and remains the principal unit of local government. In Ulster, which remained unconquered until the beginning of the seventeenth century, the county was not used as the leading unit of local government until the Plantation. The importance of the county was confirmed by the subsequent mapping of Ireland which established the county system.

The barony

The barony was an important county subdivision. The origin of the barony remains obscure. However, the name was already in use by the sixteenth century, many baronies relating to the former Gaelic lordships. A barony could occupy part of two counties, in which case it was known as a half-barony in each.

From the sixteenth to the nineteenth century the barony was used in surveys, censuses etc. The various valuations of Ireland carried out in the nineteenth century are organized and published by barony and it was not until the reorganization of local government in 1898 that the barony was excluded as an important territorial division. Researchers should note that the areas of baronies changed over time.

The parish

The parish in the past has been both an ecclesiastical and a civil unit. In England and Wales it was developed as a unit of local government by the Crown and grew in importance as the manor declined. In Ireland, until the nineteenth century, the parish was responsible for the relief of poverty, the collection of tithe and the provision of recruits for the army.

Since the sixteenth century the Church of Ireland and the Roman Catholic Church have had two separate parochial structures. The Church of Ireland retained the medieval parochial divisions. Therefore the civil parishes used in early censuses, tax records and maps are almost identical to the Church of Ireland parishes. The creation of new Catholic parishes in the nineteenth century means that the registers relevant to a particular area may be split between two or more civil parishes.

It is important to remember that both the Church of Ireland and the Roman Catholic Church have modified their parish system in response to social change and shifts of population. Therefore it is worth seeking the advice of local clergy or checking out parish histories to find out if a particular church has been in more than one parish.

The poor law union

In February 1837, the government introduced a 'Bill for the more effectual relief of the destitute poor in Ireland'. The Bill, which became law on 1 July 1838, established a system of indoor relief through a series of workhouses into which the destitute could be interned out of sight behind the workhouse walls. In England the units on which the poor law was administered were civil parishes, but in Ireland, where the parishes had become outdated owing to changes in population and settlement, the poor law unions were devised. The unions ignored traditional divisions, such as the county, barony and parish, and were centred on market towns where workhouses were built. One hundred and thirty-seven unions were created, varying considerably in size: the largest ones were in the west of Ireland and the small ones in the eastern part of Ulster where the population was most dense.

The poor law union was adopted as the district on which civil registration was based when it was first introduced on a very limited scale in 1845. Researchers wishing to consult valuation or census records will need to know in which poor law union a particular townland is located. This can be done by means of the *Alphabetical Index* held in the Public Search Room of the main archival institutions. Researchers should be aware that major cities like Belfast and Dublin were incorporated within more than one poor law union.

District electoral divisions

Poor law unions were in turn subdivided into district electoral divisions for electoral purposes. Census records are numerically arranged by district electoral division (DED). Therefore before consulting the 1901 and 1911 census returns, you must establish in which DED the relevant townland or street is situated. This can be done by consulting the *Alphabetical Index* which is held in the public search room of the major archives and by many libraries throughout Ireland.

Ordnance Survey maps

Before the nineteenth century various parts of Ireland had been mapped by landowners in the interests of estate management. Surveyors were employed to measure and plot each part of the estate in varying degrees of detail depending on the amount of money available. It was not until the early nineteenth century, when the idea of having a new land tax was introduced, that the government decided that it required the whole of Ireland to be mapped on a large scale in order to show the land boundaries more accurately.

The Ordnance Survey Office was established in 1824 to carry out a survey of the entire island to update land valuations for land taxation purposes. By 1846, the entire island had been surveyed at a scale of six inches to one mile. Ireland was the first country in the world to be entirely mapped at such a detailed scale. Nevertheless, when the publication of the first edition of the six-inch map was completed, revision of the early six-inch maps had already begun. These Ordnance Survey maps are a faithful record of the landscape for this period of the nineteenth century. For the first time the boundaries of all townlands, civil parishes, baronies and counties were delineated.

Ordnance Survey maps are available at the NAI, NLI and PRONI and are invaluable if you want to become familiar with the landscape in which your ancestor lived. The Irish townland maps can also be purchased online at www.pasthomes.com.

3 Civil Registration

IVIL OR STATE REGISTRATION of all births, deaths and marriages began in Ireland on 1 January 1864. Non-Catholic marriages, including Protestant and Jewish marriages as well as those conducted in a government registry office, were required in law to be registered from 1 April 1845.

Civil registration followed the administrative divisions created by the Poor Law Act of 1838. This Act divided counties into poor law unions: each of these had a workhouse where paupers were accommodated. The poor law unions were in turn subdivided into dispensary districts, each with its own medical officer.

Under civil registration the area covered by a poor law union was used as the basis of each superintendent registrar's district, while the dispensary districts corresponded to the registrars' districts. In some cases the medical officer also served as the registrar. In overall charge of registration was the Registrar General in Dublin. Certified copies of all registers compiled locally were sent to his office and, from these, indexes covering the whole of Ireland were produced.

Birth certificates

The first significant evidence of the life an individual born since 1864 is his or her birth certificate. From this we can learn where a person was born, the names of the parents, the maiden name of the mother, and the occupation of the father. This gives the researcher many important clues with which to move back to a previous generation.

Birth certificates normally give the name of the child, but in some cases only the sex is recorded, i.e., the child had not been given a name by the time the birth was registered. The name and residence of the father are registered. Although the latter is usually the same as the place of birth of the child, in some cases it will show that the father was working abroad or in another part of Ireland when the child was born. The mother's maiden name is provided as well as her first name. Finally, the name and address of the informant recorded, together with his or her qualification to sign. This person will usually be the father or mother or someone present at the birth, such as a midwife or even the child's grandmother.

It is important to treat the dates on Irish birth certificates with a degree of caution. As a general rule, the younger the child was when registered, the more accurate the birth date written in the official register. The longer families waited to register the child the more chance that the date given is inaccurate. Families were also prepared to change the date of birth if the child was more than three months old to avoid paying the late registration penalty.

Marriage certificates

Civil records of marriage normally give fuller information than birth and death certificates, and are the most useful of the civil records. Information on the individuals getting married includes their name, age, status, and occupation. The names and occupations of their fathers are also given. The church, the officiating minister and the witnesses to the ceremony are named. In most cases the exact age of the parties is not registered, and the entry will simply read 'full age' (i.e., over 21) or 'minor' (i.e., under 21). If the father of one of the parties was no longer living this may be indicated in the marriage certificate, but in many cases it is not. The fact that marriage certificates had to be filed within three days of the marriage ceremony means that marriage dates are generally accurate.

Death certificates

Civil records of death in Ireland are sadly rather uninformative. The name of the deceased is given together with the date, place and cause of death, marital status, the age of death, and occupation. The name and address of the informant is also recorded. Usually this is the person present at the time of the death, who may be a close family member, or even an employee or servant.

The indexes

Indexes to civil marriages 1845–63 are handwritten, but thereafter all indexes are printed. From 1864 to 1877 indexes for births, marriages and deaths consist of a single yearly volume covering the whole of Ireland. Records for the years 1878 to 1903 are divided into four quarters ending March, June, September and December. It is therefore necessary to check the index for each quarter in any one year. Births which were registered late are at the back of the index for each year. From 1903 to 1927, in 1933, and from 1966 to 1995 births reverted to being indexed annually. In all years indexed annually, late registrations are given after 'Z'. The name of the superintendent registrar's district is also given, followed by the volume number and page number of the master copies of the registers in Dublin.

General Register Office, Dublin

The General Register Office (Oifig An Ard-Chlaraitheora) is the civil repository for records relating to births, death and marriages in the Republic of Ireland.

The following records are held by the GRO:

◆ Registers of all births registered in the whole of Ireland from 1 January 1864 to 31 December 1921, and in Ireland (excluding Northern Ireland) after 1921

◆ Registers of all deaths registered in the whole of Ireland from 1 January 1864 to 31 December 1921, and in Ireland (excluding Northern Ireland) after 1921

◆ Registers of all marriages registered in the whole of Ireland from 1 April 1845 to 31 December 1863, except those celebrated by the Roman Catholic clergy

◆ Registers of all marriages registered in the whole of Ireland from 1 January 1864 to 31 December 1921, and in Ireland (excluding Northern Ireland) after 1921

◆ Registers of births at sea of children one of whose parents was Irish registered from 1 January 1864 to 31 December 1921 and of children one of whose parents was born in the Republic of Ireland registered after 1921

◆ Register of deaths at sea of Irish-born persons registered from 1 January 1864 to 31 December 1921, and after 1921 of Irish-born persons other than those born in Northern Ireland

◆ Registers of births of children of Irish parents certified by British consuls abroad from 1 January 1864 to 31 December 1921

◆ Registers of deaths of Irish-born persons certified by British Consuls abroad from 1 January 1864 to 31 December 1921

◆ Register of marriages celebrated in Dublin by the late Rev. J. F. G. Schulze, Minister of the German Protestant Church, Poolbeg Street, Dublin, from 1806 to 1837, inclusive

◆ Registers under the Births, Deaths and Marriages (Army) Act, 1879

◆ Adopted Children Register – legal adoptions registered in the Republic of Ireland on or after 10 July 1953

◆ Birth and death registers under the Defence (Amendment) (No 2) Act, 1960

◆ Registers of certain births and deaths occurring outside the State (The Births, Deaths and Marriages Registration Act, 1972, Sec 4)

◆ Register of certain Lourdes Marriages (Marriages Act, 1972, Sec 2)

◆ Registers of stillbirths registered in the Republic of Ireland from 1 January 1995 (certified copies available to parents only)

Indexes are currently in a manual format so accurate dates are required. Three types of index contain entries relating to either birth, death or marriage records and cover the following periods:

◆ Birth indexes – 1864 onwards

◆ Death indexes – 1864 onwards

◆ Marriage indexes –1845 onwards

Only the indexes are available for public inspection, not the records themselves. The Public Office and Research Room are open from Monday to Friday (excluding public holidays) from 9.30 am to 4.30 pm for the purpose of searching the indexes to birth, death and marriage records and obtaining certificates. A particular search covering a maximum of 5 years costs €1.90: a general search for one day covering all years costs €15.24.

The General Register Office is located at Joyce House, 8/11 Lombard Street, Dublin 2, Ireland. Applications for certificates can be made in person, by post, by telephone or online (www.grioreland.ie/applu_for_a_cert.htm).

General Register Office, Belfast, and district registrar's offices

The General Register Office (GRO) in Belfast holds the original birth and death registers recorded by the local district registrars for Northern Ireland from 1864. Marriage registers are available from 1922. The following computerized indexes to the civil registers are available:

◆ Birth indexes – 1864 onwards

◆ Death indexes – 1864 onwards

◆ Marriage indexes – 1845 onwards

A general search of records assisted by members of GRO staff for any period of years and any number of entries costs £24 per hour.

If you wish to search the indexes yourself (only indexes are available for public inspection, not the registers themselves) it is possible to visit the GRO if you have arranged a time and date in advance. An index search costs £10 for a period not exceeding six hours. This includes four verifications of items found in the indexes, with the option of further verifications at £2.50 each. A full certified copy of a birth, death or marriage certificate costs £11.

The GRO also holds records of a more specialized nature. These include:

◆ Records of still births occurring in Northern Ireland on or after 1 January 1961

◆ Records of persons adopted under orders made by courts in Northern Ireland on or after 1 January 1931

◆ Records of births at sea of children who were registered on or after 1 January 1922 one of whose parents was born in Northern Ireland

◆ Records of deaths at sea of persons born in Northern Ireland where death was registered on or after 1 January 1922

◆ Records of births of children whose father was born in Northern Ireland, deaths and marriages registered on or after 1 January 1927 by way of the Births, Deaths and Marriages (Army) Act 1879

◆ Records of births of children of Northern Ireland parents born abroad and registered by British consuls on or after 1 January 1922

◆ Records of deaths of Northern Ireland persons registered by British consuls abroad on or after 1 January 1922

◆ Records of marriages of Northern Ireland persons registered by British consuls abroad on or after 1 January 1923

◆ Records of births, deaths and marriages of Northern Ireland persons registered by the British High Commissioner in Commonwealth countries on or after 1 January 1950

◆ Certified copies of certificates (with translations) relating to marriages of persons from Northern Ireland in certain foreign countries according to the laws of these countries, without the presence of a British consular officer

◆ Records of deaths of persons born in Northern Ireland who died on war service between 1939 and 1948

The GRO is located at Oxford House, 49–55 Chichester Street, Belfast BT1 4HL. Applications for certificates can be made in person, by post, by telephone (028 9025 2000) or online (www.groni.gov.uk). Searches will be made in the year quoted plus the two years either side unless a wider search is requested. A further fee will be required for each extra five years searched. Personal applications are processed within three working days; postal or telephone applications are processed within eight working days.

Although indexes to civil marriages registers for Northern Ireland are available at the GRO from 1845, the original registers are located at the district registrar's offices at local councils. Applications for marriage certificates can be made directly to them or through the GRO in Belfast.

Church of Latter-Day Saints

From 1948 the Church of the Latter-Day Saints (LDS), or Mormons, began microfilming documentary material in Ireland. The most important resources acquired at that time were the registers of births, deaths and marriages as well as the indexes to these records held in the Registrar General's Office, Custom House, Dublin. Unfortunately the Mormons were not able to complete the filming of all registers before work was suspended.

The LDS collection of microfilms of civil registers and indexes contains:

◆ Birth indexes – 1864–1959

◆ Birth registers – 1864 to first quarter 1880; 1900–1913

◆ Marriage indexes – 1845–1959

◆ Marriage registers – 1845–70

◆ Death indexes – 1864–1959

◆ Death registers – 1864–70

It is important to note that, although there are gaps in the birth registers, microfilm copies of the actual official registers are available to researchers. This is a vital resource, because in the General Register Offices in Dublin, Belfast and London the public have no right of access to the original records. In addition, some parts of the early years of birth registrations appear in the LDS *International Genealogical Index*, which is searchable online (www.familysearch.org/), and the 2002 edition of the LDS CD set *British Isles Vital Records* includes an index to birth registrations from 1864 to 1875.

Access to microfilmed copies of the indexes and registers is also free of charge at any of the LDS Family History Centres. The Family History Library catalogue is the best way to find collections in the Family History Library. It is usual to search by place to find the records available for where your ancestors lived. The records are listed by country, county, or civil parish, depending on the nature of the records. Within each locality, the records are organized by topic – in this case 'Civil registration'.

An excellent introduction and guide to civil registration in Ireland is Catherine Blumsom's *Civil Registration of Births, Deaths and Marriages in Ireland: A Practical Approach*, published by the Ulster Historical Foundation.

Census Returns and Old Age Pension Claims

THE FIRST GOVERNMENT-ORGANISED CENSUS IN IRELAND was carried out in 1821 (twenty years before any similar enumeration in the rest of the British Isles), an unsuccessful attempt having being made eight years earlier. Thereafter a census was taken every ten years until 1911. These census returns gave names, ages, occupations and relationships to the heads of households as well as acreage of land and the number of storeys in the house.

At first glance, Irish census returns would seem to be an obvious place for family historians to begin their search. The early census records were held by the Public Record Office in Dublin and were an invaluable source for Victorian genealogists. According to the *28th Report of the Deputy Keeper of the Public Records in Ireland, 1896*, 'The Census Returns of 1813, 1821, 1831–34, 1841 and 1851, are of record here transferred at different times from their places of original deposit. Their accessibility to the public has proved of incalculable value in inquiries concerning title and pedigree and the tracing of next-of-kin and heirs-at law.'

Unfortunately, the census returns from 1861 to 1891 were destroyed by government order, and those from 1821 to 1851 were destroyed in an explosion and fire in the Public Record Office of Ireland, Dublin, during the Irish Civil War.

Once you have located the area in which your ancestors lived it is then a matter of pinpointing the records that have survived for that particular area.

1821 census

This census was organised by townland, civil parish, barony and county and took place on 28 May 1821. Almost all the original returns were destroyed in 1922, with only a few volumes surviving for Counties Fermanagh (PRONI MIC 5A and MIC 15A), Cavan, Galway, Meath and King's County (Offaly). You can find call numbers for all of these in the *Pre-1901 Census Material* catalogue in the NAI. They are also on microfilm (MFGI-34).

An original enumerator's notebook, covering eight townlands in Kilmore parish, has also survived and is held in the Armagh Public Library, with a copy in PRONI (T/450). For Monaghan, 1821, see *Thrift Abstracts*, National Archives of Ireland (NAI), also *Clogher Record*, 1991.

Cavan census returns for the parishes of Annageliffe, Ballymacue, Castlerahan, Castleterra, Crosserlough, Denn, Drumlumman, Drung, Kilbride, Kilmore, Kinawley, Larah, Lavery, Lurgan, Mullagh and Munterconnaght are available on LDS films LDS 597154–158.

1831–4 census

Once again this census was organised by townland, civil parish, barony and county. It also includes the name, age, occupation and religion of the occupants. No original returns survive, but in 1834 the Commissioners of Public Instruction, Ireland, made copies of the original returns, and information survives for Co. Londonderry at PRONI:

◆ Barony of Coleraine – MIC 5A/6

◆ City of Londonderry – MIC 5A/6 to 7

◆ Barony of Loughlinsholin – MIC 5A/8

◆ Barony of Tirkeeran – MIC 5A/9

The census returns for Londonderry are also available at the NAI. You can find the call numbers in the *Pre-1901 Census Material* catalogue. An index, compiled by the Derry Inner City Trust, is also available at the NAI on microfiche.

The Commissioners of Public Instruction also instructed clergy of all denominations to conduct censuses in their areas in 1834. Few of these returns are available. The 1834 census of Granard parish in Co. Longford, listing heads of household, is held by the NLI (Pos. 4237). Returns for seven civil parishes in Co. Kerry have been published in the *Journal of the Kerry Archaeological and Historical Society* (1974–5), and those for Templebredin in Counties Limerick and Tipperary in the *North Muster Antiquarian Journal*, vol. 17 (1975). The censuses for Tallanstown, Co. Louth, published in the *Journal of the Co. Louth Archaeological Society*, vol. 14 (1957), and Kilcumreragh in Counties Offaly and Westmeath, on microfilm at the NLI (Pos. 1994), appear to be part of this survey.

1841 census

The government census taken on 6 June 1841 followed the same general pattern as that of 1831; however, the householders themselves compiled the returns rather than government enumerators. Unfortunately, very little has survived. Some abstracts exist for Co. Monaghan, *Thrift Abstracts*, NAI. For Cavan, returns survive for part of the parish of Killeshandra and for some households in Counties Cork, Fermanagh and Waterford are held in the NAI. You can find the call numbers in the *Pre-1901 Census Material* catalogue.

1851 census

The comments above on transcripts of the 1841 census also apply to 1851. Taken on 30 March 1851, this government census added a column for religious affiliation. Most of the surviving returns relate to Co. Antrim and the townland of Clonee in Co. Fermanagh, held at PRONI (MIC 5A/11-26) and the NAI (call numbers are available in the *Pre-1901 Census Material* catalogue).

There are also individual census returns for various parts of
Northern Ireland in PRONI MIC/15A. Some extracts survive for
Co. Monaghan, *Thrift Abstracts*, NAI. Extracts for Aglish, Portnascully
and Rathkieran in Co. Kilkenny are at the Genealogical Office (Ms
684). The NAI also has lists of heads of households for Cromac
Ward, Belfast (Cen 1851/19) and the city of Dublin (Cen 1851/18/1-
2).

Abstracts from the 1841 and 1851 censuses are also available on
a CD-ROM, *Irish Source Records*, published by the Genealogical
Publishing Company (www.genealogical.com/products/
Irish%20Source%20Records/7275.html). The *1851 Dublin City
Census, Chart's Index of Heads of Household* CD-ROM compiled and
edited by Seán Magee (Eneclann, 2001) is also recommended.

1861, 1871, 1881 and 1891 censuses

The census records for 1861 to 1891 were destroyed by order of the
government during the First World War.

1901 census

On 31 March 1901, a census was taken of the whole island of Ireland.
The original returns are deposited at the NAI; microfilm copies of
the returns for Northern Ireland are available at PRONI. The census
records:

◆ names;

◆ relationship to the head of the household;

◆ religion;

◆ literacy;

◆ occupation;

◆ age;

◆ marital status;

◆ county of birth;

◆ ability to speak English or Irish.

Every town, village and townland in Ireland is represented and those inhabitants who were at home on 31 March 1901 are listed.

A catalogue of the original census returns is held at the NAI on the open shelves in the Reading Room. Each county is listed in a separate volume. The records are numerically arranged by district electoral division (DED) and held in bound volumes. Before consulting the 1901 census returns, you must establish in which DED the relevant townland or street is situated. The DED was a subdivision of the old poor law union and was used for electoral purposes. The DED, with a number attached, can be found in the 1901 *Townland Index*, which is available on the shelves of the Search Room. Simply look up the relevant townland, village or town and you will find it listed along with the barony and poor law union.

Within each DED the townlands are arranged alphabetically and numerically. In order to request the returns for a particular townland you must include the name of the county, the number of the DED and the number of the townland.

The 1901 census is available on microfilm at PRONI under reference MIC/354. Once again it is necessary to find out the relevant DED. This can be done by consulting the 1901 *Townland Index*, which is available on the shelves of the Search Room. Each DED is listed in a series of calendars which will give you the appropriate reel number.

1911 census

The 1911 census was taken on 1 April of that year and includes, in addition to the information in the 1901 census, the number of years a wife had been married, the number of children born and the number still living. This census is not yet available at PRONI because of the more restrictive UK 'hundred year closure rule' on access, but microfilms of the original census returns can be viewed at the NAI.

In order to locate the relevant DED number, the townland, town or street number it is necessary to consult the *1911 Census* catalogue, available on the open shelves in the NAI. Sometimes this number corresponds with the number used in 1901, but in many cases it does not. The number used in 1911 is usually close to the 1901 number. If the 1911 DED number cannot be found, help should be sought from the Search Room staff.

It is important to realise that there were boundary changes in townlands and DEDs between 1901 and 1911; an official Parliamentary Paper listing these changes was published. Unlike the 1901 census returns, which are held in large bound volumes, those for 1911 are unbound and stored in folders within boxes.

1901 and 1911 censuses online

Accessing information from the Irish census returns from the census records can be time-consuming for researchers because the information is accessible only by townland or street, not by individual name. This means that descendants of city-dwellers, in particular, can have a very hard time tracing their ancestors, as people in cities tended to move around a lot. It is also difficult to trace an ancestor if they worked as a servant, boarded in lodgings or lived in an institution such as a school, religious community, police barracks or workhouse.

On 6 December 2005, John O'Donoghue, Irish Minister for Arts, Sports and Tourism, announced the signing of an agreement between the NAI and the Library and Archives Canada, which will have great significance for all researchers with Irish roots. Under this agreement the Irish census records for 1901 and 1911 will be digitised, indexed over a three-year period and placed online for free access, making it considerably easier for the more than 70 million people of Irish descent around the world to retrace their families and heritage.

The Irish Census Project will digitise over 3000 census microfilm reels, and create two indexes linked to the digital images: a topographical index based on townland/street within DEDs, and a nominal index to every individual listed in both censuses. Unfortunately no date for release has as yet been announced.

Old age pension claims

It is worth checking old age pension search forms, as they contain extracts from the 1841 and 1851 censuses, which were almost

completely destroyed. The old age pension was introduced on
1 January 1909 for those over 70 years of age. For many born before
1864, when the state registration of births began in Ireland, it was
necessary to submit a form and to pay for a search to be made of
the 1841 and 1851 censuses in order to prove their entitlement to the
pension. The individual claim forms completed by or on behalf of
the applicant are known as 'green forms'. They contain the applicant's
name, contact address, age, parents' names and address at the time of
the 1841 or 1851 census. The result of the search was added in the
form of a brief statement as to whether or not the applicant's name
had been located in the census. The green forms for Ireland are held
at the NAI under reference CEN/S/8.

Another form of evidence related to the old age pension returns are
'form 37s', which were submitted by local pensions offices. These
include the applicant's name, stated age, parents' names and address at
the time of the census. Details of the search were added to the form,
and each claim was bound according to barony. A series of volumes
relating to claimants born in Cavan and neighbouring counties, is
deposited in the NAI (M.3168/1-267). Those for Northern Ireland
are held at PRONI (T/550/2-37).

A partial index is available on microfiche (reference MF/9/1/1-9),
but its entries relate to the LDS microfilm copy and do not always
correspond to the originals. Josephine Masterson of Indianapolis,
USA, compiled a volume based mainly on surviving old age
pension claims. This is entitled *Ireland 1841/1851 Census Abstracts
(Northern Ireland)*.

5 Census Substitutes

Fiants of the Tudor sovereigns, 1521–1603

THE IRISH FIANTS OF THE TUDOR SOVEREIGNS Henry VIII, Edward VI, Philip and Mary and Elizabeth I have been called the single most important source for sixteenth-century Irish history. Fiants were the warrants issued to command the drawing up of letters-patent, the formal royal letters by which grants of land, official appointments, pardons, etc., were made, but in the Tudor period the drawing up of the actual letters-patent was often neglected, and the fiants remained the basic record.

The uniqueness of the information contained in the fiants encouraged the staff in the newly established Public Record Office of Ireland in Dublin to publish calendars of these fiants. Ingeniously, they got the calendars published as appendices in the steady stream of annual reports published by the office in the years 1857–90 (Reports nos 11–13, 15–18 of the Deputy Keeper of the Public Records of Ireland). The attention of the scholarly world was drawn to the quality of the information available in the Irish fiants by the publication of reprints of the calendars for the years 1521–1603 by Edmund Burke in 1994. These serve as very adequate substitutes for the original records destroyed in the Public Record Office of Ireland.

When Irish chiefs were granted pardons under the 'surrender and regrant' policy they often listed scores of members of their extended families as well as kerns and gallowglasses (mercenary soldiers), horsemen and yeomen, husbandmen, tenants and even, on occasion, cottiers. Individuals were identified with their full names, often with specific locations.

Calendars of patent rolls from the reigns of James I and Charles I

The patent rolls were the most important records in the chancery archives. On them were enrolled copies of letters-patent, which granted crown lands on lease, surrenders and regrants to Irish lords, royal letters and many other documents of which it was thought necessary to keep a record. A roll generally contains the record of one year.

The original Irish patent rolls were also destroyed in the Public Record Office, Dublin, in 1922. Fortunately, some of the material had been published in calendar form. Printed calendars have survived for the patent rolls of James I and the early part of the reign of Charles I. These contain the names of the native Irish who received grants of land or were pardoned for transgressions committed during the years 1603–1633. The calendars also include the names of Scots in Ulster who were given grants of denization to enable them to enjoy the same rights as English subjects. This was particularly important in matters of inheritance. The Reverend David Stewart, a Presbyterian minister and a very active local historian, extracted from the printed calendars the names of about a thousand Scots who were recorded as having been granted denization.

The *Calendar of the Patent Rolls of the Reign of James I* was prepared under the direction of the Irish Record Commission prior to 1830 and was printed before the Commission closed. The Irish Manuscripts Commission published a facsimile of the printed calendar in 1966, but this publication is now out of print. Unfortunately no personal and place name index to this calendar has as yet been published.

Seventeenth-century muster rolls

A muster roll was a list of able-bodied men who were capable of military service. These men were armed at their own expense. The muster rolls for 1642–3 were compiled following the outbreak of the 1641 rebellion and represent the settler response to the crisis.

Muster rolls contain lists of the principal landlords in Ulster, and the names of the men they could assemble in an emergency. The Armagh County Museum copy is available in the NLI (Positive microfilm 206). PRONI also holds copies on microfilm (MIC/15A/52 – 53 & 73). The following list indicates what survives for each county:

Co. Antrim

◆ Muster Roll, 1630–31, PRONI D/1759/3C/3
◆ Muster Roll, 1642, PRONI T/3726/2

Co. Armagh

◆ Muster Roll, 1631, T/934

Co. Cavan

◆ Muster Roll, 1630, PRONI T/934; BL add. Ms. 4770
◆ Muster Roll for Cavan, *Breifny*, 1977/8, also NLI Pos.206

Co. Donegal

◆ Muster Roll for Donegal, *Donegal Annual*, vol. X, no. 2, NLI Pos.206, PRONI, D/1759/3C/2 & T/808/15164. Also searchable online.

Co. Down

◆ Muster Roll for Co. Down, 1630, PRONI D/1759/3C/1
◆ Muster Roll for Co. Down, 1642–1643, PRONI T/563
◆ Muster Rolls for Donaghadee, Co. Down, 1642, PRONI T/3726/2

Co. Fermanagh

◆ Muster Roll, 1630, PRONI T/510/2
◆ Muster Roll, 1631, PRONI T/934

Co. Londonderry

◆ Muster Roll, 1620–22, PRONI T/510/2
◆ Muster Roll, 1630–31, PRONI D/1759/3C/2

Co. Monaghan

◆ Muster Roll, PRONI, D/1759/3C/1

Co. Tyrone

◆ Muster Roll, 1630, PRONI T458/7
◆ Muster Roll, 1631, PRONI T/934
◆ Muster Rolls, 1631, 1666 PRONI T/716

A muster roll for Ulster for 1630 is held by the British Museum (Add. Ms 4770). Copies are held by PRONI (MIC/339) and NLI (n.12. p.296), and by major libraries such as the Linen Hall Library and Central Library, Belfast.

Depositions, 1641

The depositions of 1641 are the collected accounts of witnesses to the robberies and murders that took place during the rebellion of that year. Eight Protestant clergymen, led by Henry Jones, Dean of Kilmore, were empowered to take evidence during two commissions in December 1641 and January 1642. In 1652, following Cromwell's subjugation of the country, a High Court of Justice was established to collect evidence for the trials of those who had risen against the settlers.

Most of the witnesses were English settlers and their occupations ranged from 'gentlemen' to 'tanner', 'tailor' and 'inn keeper'. They named their attackers, or those rumoured to have taken part in the rising, and the depositions provide rare documentary evidence of the native Irish families who had once dominated the country. The original depositions for Counties Antrim, Armagh, Cavan, Down, Monaghan and Tyrone are deposited in the library of Trinity College, Dublin, reference Ms 837. Copies of the 1641 depositions are available at PRONI, reference D/1923, T/2706/8 and MIC/8/1. Copies are also held in the NAI, reference n.4579p.4545. Trinity College recently announced a 1 million Euro three-year digital imaging project which will make the depositions available online.

Poll tax, 1660s

The Poll Tax was levied at irregular intervals mainly to provide money for military purposes. An Ordinance of the General Convention dated 24 April 1660 stated 'every person above the age of fifteen years of either sex . . . under the degree or quality of yeoman, or farmer yeoman, or farmer's wife or widow shall pay twelve pence'. The sums payable by gentlemen, esquires, knights, barons, earls and others were then specified in an ascending scale. The Poll Tax returns give detailed facts about individuals quite unique in surviving seventeenth-century records.

See the following:

Co. Armagh

◆ 1660 Poll Tax returns, PRONI MIC 15A/74; RCB Ms Libr.48

Co. Donegal

◆ 1660 Poll Tax returns, PRONI MIC/15A/76 and T/808/15005

Co. Down

◆ 1660 Poll Tax returns, PRONI MIC 15A/72
◆ 1698 Poll Tax returns, Newry and Mourne, PRONI T/1046

Co. Fermanagh

◆ 1660 Poll Tax returns, PRONI MIC 15A/80

Co. Londonderry

◆ 1669 Poll Tax returns, PRONI MIC 15A/82

Co. Tyrone

◆ 1696 and 1698 Manuscript notes and details of Poll Tax payments, PRONI T/808/15095

Dublin

◆ Poll tax assessments for the city of Dublin, 1696 and 1699, NAI M.2469

Books of survey and distribution

The books of survey and distribution were compiled in the course of the Restoration land settlement of the 1660s and 1670s. They are laid out on a barony and parish basis and include a record of land ownership before the Cromwellian and Williamite confiscations as well as the names of the individuals to whom the land was distributed. They were used to impose the acreable rent called the Quit Rent, which was payable yearly on lands granted under the terms of the Acts of Settlement and Explanation.

A fire in 1711 in the Surveyors' and Auditor General's Office destroyed the office copies of the books of survey and distribution, but fortunately, duplicate copies have survived. One of these sets, known as the Taylor Books after the official who helped in their compilation, is now in the Royal Irish Academy. These consist of 28 volumes although Counties Roscommon, Mayo, Galway and Clare are missing. A set can be found in the *Annesley Papers* at PRONI and another set is held by the NAI (n. 4093, p. 3764). The Irish Manuscripts Commission has published four volumes of the books. These are for Roscommon (1949), Mayo (1956), Galway (1962) and Clare (1967).

Census of Ireland, c. 1659

Sir William Petty's surveyors probably made the census of 1659. Petty, described by Samuel Pepys as 'the most intelligent man I know', arrived in Ireland in 1652 as physician-general to Cromwell's armies. He soon abandoned medicine in order to concentrate on cartography, surveying and economics and was made responsible for mapping all the 2,800,000 acres of land confiscated after the Cromwellian victory in Ireland. It was the first systematic survey of Ireland, requiring 1000 assistants, and in many ways was a forerunner of the Ordnance Survey.

The census of 1659 contains only the names of those with title to land (tituladoes) and the total number of English and Irish resident in each townland (Scots were usually counted with English). Five counties, Cavan, Galway, Mayo, Tyrone and Wicklow, are not covered. An edition of the census by Seamus Pender was published in 1939 by the Stationery Office, Dublin, on behalf of the Irish Manuscripts Commission. This includes a breakdown of the figures for each county and an index of both personal names and place names. Copies of Petty's census are held by the National Library, NLI 6551, and on microfilm by PRONI, MIC/15/A and in T/808.

Subsidy rolls, 1663–66

Subsidy rolls list the nobility, clergy and laity who paid grants in aid to the Crown. The surviving lists, relating largely to Ulster, are made up of those of means in the community who were subject to the payment of subsidies, which then formed the government's main method of direct taxation. They include the amount paid and the status of the person.

An index to the names of persons listed in the 1663 subsidy roll is available on the shelves of the Public Search Room at PRONI and a copy is available under reference T/307. Copies are also available at the NLI (Ms 9584/5) and NAI (M 2745).

The following list will give a better indication of what is available for each county:

Co. Antrim

◆ 1666 Subsidy Roll, PRONI T/808/14889

Co. Armagh

◆ 1634 Subsidy Roll, NAI M.2471, 2475; Representative Church Body Ms Libr 48

Co. Down

◆ 1663 Subsidy Roll, PRONI T/307; NAI M.2745; NLI Mss.9584 with index 9585

Co. Fermanagh

◆ 1662 Subsidy Roll, PRONI T/808/15068; NLI Ms 9583
◆ 1663 (Enniskillen town only)

Co. Tyrone

◆ 1664 Subsidy Roll, PRONI T/283/D/1; NLI Ms 9583
◆ 1665, 1668, Subsidy Rolls, Armagh Museum, n.12 p.206
◆ 1667, 1668 Subsidy Rolls, NAI, M.2470

Co. Cork

◆ 1662–8, Extracts for Subsidy Rolls, NAI M.2636: 2643
◆ 1662–7, Extracts from Subsidy Rolls of Condons and Glangibbons, NAI M.4968

Dublin

◆ 1634, Subsidy Roll, NAI M.2469

Hearth money rolls

Arranged by county and parish, these list the name of the householder and the number of hearths on which he was taxed, at the rate of 2 shillings on every hearth or fireplace. The tax was collected over areas known as 'walks' and based on the town. The 'Lisburn Walk', for example, covered a large area of the south of Co. Antrim and not merely Lisburn town.

The largest dwelling on which hearth money was paid was that of the Earl of Donegal at Carrickfergus (40 hearths), closely followed by that of Sir George Rawdon at Lisburn (39 hearths), both in Co. Antrim. Its unpopularity led to its abolition in England and Wales after the Glorious Revolution of 1688. In Ireland it continued to be levied until the act of Union in 1800. The original Heath Money Rolls were destroyed in the Four Courts in 1922. Fortunately the Presbyterian Historical Society of Ireland had preserved copies of the rolls for the mid-1660s and copies are now held by the major archives. See the following:

Co. Antrim

◆ 1666 Hearth Money Roll, NAI M.2745
◆ 1669 Hearth Money Roll, PRONI T/307 and MIC/15A/72
◆ Parish of Carnmoney, Hearthmoney Roll of 1669, in *Three Centuries in South East Antrim*, by Rev. H.St.J. Clarke

Co. Armagh

◆ 1664 Hearth Money Roll, PRONI T/604/and MIC/15A/74
◆ 1664, 1665 Armagh Hearth Money Rolls, extracts, NAI M.2471
◆ 1740 Hearth Money Roll, list of names in Armagh, Armagh Public Library
◆ County Armagh Hearthmoney Rolls, 1664, edited by the Rev. L.P. Murray, in *Archivium Hibernicum*, vol. 8, pp.121–202 (1936)

Co. Cavan

◆ 1664 Hearth Money Roll, parishes of Killeshandra, Kildallan, Killenagh, Templeport, Tomregan, PRONI MIC/15A/82

Co. Donegal

◆ 1665 Hearth Money Roll, GO 538, NL Ms.9583, PRONI T/307/ D and T/808/15003

◆ Hearthmoney Rolls of County Donegal, 1665, edited by R.J. Dickson, in *Journal of the County Donegal Historical Society*, vol. 1, nos 2, 3 (1949)

◆ 1665 Hearth Money Roll for the Parish of Raphoe, PRONI T/ 295–296

Co. Fermanagh

◆ 1665–6 Hearth Money Roll, PRONI T808/15066

◆ 1665–7 Hearth Money Roll for the Parish of Devenish, PRONI T/265

◆ Hearthmoney Rolls for Enniskillen, 1665 and 1666, in *Enniskillen, Parish and Town*, by W.H. Dundas (1913)

Co. Londonderry

◆ 1663 Hearth Money Roll, PRONI T/307

◆ Hearthmoney Rolls, Parish of Aghanloo, 1663, in *Historical Gleanings from County Derry*, by Samuel Martin (Dublin 1955)

Co. Lough

◆ Hearthmoney Rolls for the Parishes of Kilsaran, Gernonstown, Stabannan, Manfieldstown and Dromiskin, 1664, 1666–7, in *History of Kilsaran Union of Parishes in the County of Louth*, by Rev. James B. Leslie (Dundalk, 1908)

Co. Monaghan

◆ 1663/65 Hearth Money Roll, in *A History of Monaghan*, by D.C. Rushe

Co. Sligo

◆ 1663 Transcript of a Hearth Money assessment of County Sligo, with an index of places, NLI Ms 2165

◆ 1664 Hearthmoney Roll, *Irish Manuscripts Commission*, 1967

Co. Tipperary

◆ 1667 Extracts from Hearth Money Rolls for County Tipperary, GO Ms 572
◆ *Tipperary's Families: Being the Hearthmoney Records for 1665–7,* edited by Thomas Laffan (Dublin, 1911)

Co. Tyrone

◆ 1664 Hearth Money Roll, PRONI T/283/D/2 and T/1365; NLI Ms 9583
◆ 1666 Hearth Money Roll, PRONI T/307 and MIC/15A/81

Co. Westmeath

◆ Hearthmoney Roll of Mullingar, *Franciscan College, Journal,* 1950
◆ Hearth Money Roll giving 'protestants and papists' in Athlone Town, 1724(?), PRONI T/1023/245

Co. Wicklow

◆ Hearthmoney Roll, 1669, GO 667; NAI m 4909
◆ Hearthmoney Rolls for County Wicklow, in *Journal of the Royal Society of Antiquaries of Ireland,* vol. 61

'Census of Protestant householders', 1740

What has generally been termed a 'census of Protestant householders' was compiled in 1740. The returns were made by the collectors of the hearth money and it has, therefore, been recently suggested that this 'census' is actually a hearth money roll. It is no more than a list of names arranged by county, barony and parish and, reflecting its supervision by the inspector responsible for collecting hearth money, it is occasionally divided into 'walks'. The original records of this survey were destroyed in Dublin in 1922 but copies survive for part of the survey in transcripts prepared by the genealogist Tension Groves. Copies are held by PRONI (T/808/15258) and the NLI (Ms 4173). A bound transcript copy is available on the open shelves of the Public Search Room at PRONI.

The religious census, 1766

In March and April 1766, Church of Ireland rectors were instructed by the government to compile complete returns of all householders in their respective parishes, showing their religion, distinguishing between Church of Ireland (Episcopalians), Roman Catholic (termed 'Papists' in the returns) and Presbyterians (or Dissenters), and giving an account of any Roman Catholic clergy active in their area. Some of the more diligent rectors listed every townland and every household, but many drew up only numerical totals of the population. All the original returns were destroyed in the Public Record Office in 1922, but extensive transcripts, again made by Tension Groves, survive for the parishes of Seapatrick, Tullynakill, Greyabbey, Inch and Kilbroney. A bound copy can be found on the shelves of the Public Search Room at PRONI.

Copies of the 1766 Householders List can also be found at the Linen Hall Library, Belfast; Armagh Museum; the Representative Church Body Library, Dublin (Ms 23); NLI (Ms 4173); and at Family History Centres across Ireland (LDS film 1279330). Some originals and transcripts are available at the Genealogical Office (GO 537). A full listing of all surviving manuscripts is available on the shelves of the Reading Room of the NAI.

Irish Tontines, 1773, 1775 and 1777

The records of the Irish Tontines of 1773, 1775 and 1777 cover 1773–1871, and list many people, with addresses. Tontines were government schemes for raising money. In return for an original investment, participants were guaranteed a yearly income for the life of a living nominee chosen by the investor – most nominated their youngest relative. The records may give details of the marriages, deaths and wills of contributors and nominees. These records are held at the National Archives, London, NDO3.

Petition of Protestant Dissenters, 1775

The Petition of Protestant Dissenters is a list of names of Dissenters (or Presbyterians) on either a parish or a congregational basis which were submitted to the government in October and November 1775.

Transcript copies are located on the shelves of PRONI under reference T/808/14977. The NLI reference is Ms 4173.

Catholic Qualification Rolls

During the eighteenth century, restrictions enacted by the Penal Laws were relaxed for those Catholics who took the Oath of Allegiance and so 'qualified'. In 1774 an Act was passed to permit the King's subjects of whatever religion to take an oath at the local assize to testify their loyalty and allegiance to him to promote peace and industry in the kingdom. Records of the more than 1500 Roman Catholics who took the oath under the 1774 Act, and subsequent Acts of 1782, 1792 and 1793, are found in the Catholic qualification rolls. The original lists were destroyed in 1922, but a transcript was published as an appendix to the *59th Deputy Keeper's Report*. Indexes to the Catholic qualification rolls, 1778–90 and 1793–6, are held in the NAI, n. 1898–9, p. 1898–9.

The flaxseed premium, 1796

In 1796, as part of a government initiative to encourage the linen industry in Ireland, free spinning-wheels or looms were granted to farmers who planted a certain acreage of their holdings with flax. The names of over 56,000 recipients of these awards have survived in printed form arranged by county and parish.

More than half the names relate to Ulster. The only copy of the book listing the names of these recipients known to exist until recently was held in the Linen Hall Library, Belfast. Another copy has now been acquired by the Irish Linen Centre in Lisburn Museum.

The Ulster Historical Foundation has indexed this source and it is available on a searchable database on the UHF website (www.ance stryireland.com). Recipients from Kerry are also available online at www.rootsweb.com/~irlker/flax1796.html. A microfiche index is available in the NAI and PRONI.

The Ulster Covenant, 1912

Prime Minister H.H. Asquith introduced the third Home Rule Bill to the House of Commons on 11 April 1912. It provided for a parliament in Dublin with limited powers, and it met with strong opposition from Ulster Unionists, who saw it as the first step to Irish independence. On 'Ulster Day', 28 September 1912, the Ulster Covenant was signed by 237,368 men and 234,046 women who pledged themselves to use 'all means which may be found necessary to defeat the present conspiracy to set up a Home Rule Parliament in Ireland'.

The Ulster Covenant signatories of 1912 are an invaluable, if underused, genealogical resource at PRONI (reference D/1098). The list includes not simply names but also street addresses, townlands, etc. The signatures have been indexed by PRONI and a searchable database is available on its website (www.PRONI.gov.uk).

Wills and Testamentary Records

O NCE THE DATE OF DEATH of an ancestor has been discovered, it is worth finding out whether they left a will. Wills contain not only the name, address and occupation of the testator, but also details of the larger family network, such as cousins and nephews. Many wills also include the addresses and occupations of the beneficiaries, witnesses and executors. It must be borne in mind, however, that the vast majority of people did not make a will. From 1540 until 1837 a will could be made by any male over the age of 14 years and by a female over the age of 12 years. After 1837, a testator had to be of full age, that is to say, 21 years or over.

Before the 1882 Married Women's Property Act married women rarely made wills as all their possessions, even their clothes, in law belonged to their husbands. Therefore, women's wills before 1883 were mostly made by widows and spinsters and even after this date they are not very numerous until the 1940s and 1950s.

One should not assume that because the family was poor members would not have made a will. Sometimes those who made a will were determined that their money or possessions went to the right person when they died. Strangely it doesn't always follow that people who were in comfortable positions left wills. People from well-to-do families sometimes disposed of their wealth before they died in order to avoid death duties.

Administration of wills

Between 1536 and 1858, the Church of Ireland was responsible for all wills and administrations in Ireland. The Probate Act of 1857 transferred probate authority from the Church of Ireland to the newly founded government probate districts. The Church of Ireland subsequently transferred their wills and administration records to the Public Record Office in Dublin. Most wills from before 1900 – some dating from the early sixteenth century – were destroyed when, in 1922, the Public Record Office was bombed during the Irish Civil War. Luckily, will indexes and administration indexes survived and copies of most wills after 1858 were preserved.

Betham's abstracts and pedigrees

In addition, Sir William Betham, as Ulster King of Arms, 1820–53, superintended the construction of alphabetical indexes and also wrote brief genealogical abstracts of almost all those wills that pre-dated 1800. He later constructed sketch pedigrees from his notes. The original notebooks in which he recorded the information are now in the NAI, and the Genealogical Office has his sketch pedigrees based on these abstracts and including later additions and amendments. The Genealogical Office transcript copy (GO 257-260) is fully alphabetical, unlike the notebooks. PRONI has in its custody a later copy of Betham's volumes of pedigrees while small 'family trees' compiled from almost all pre-1858 prerogative wills are to be found in the Burke Collection, to which there is a typescript catalogue, Index T/559.

Wills before 1858

Prior to 1858 the Church of Ireland was responsible for administering all testamentary affairs. Ecclesiastical or Consistorial Courts in each diocese were responsible for granting probate and conferring on the executors the power to administer the estate. Each court was responsible for wills and administrations in its own diocese. You can use Brian Mitchell's *A New Genealogical Atlas of Ireland*, which has county maps that associate civil parishes with Church of Ireland dioceses, to identify the diocese in which your ancestor lived. Researchers should also bear in mind that when the estate included property worth more than £5 in another diocese, responsibility for the will or administration passed to the Prerogative Court under the authority of the Archbishop of Armagh.

Indexes to those wills destroyed in 1922 are available on the shelves of the Search Rooms at PRONI and the NAI. These are useful, for although the will cannot now be produced, the index contains the name and residence of the testator and the date that the will was either made or probated. Occasionally the testator's occupation is given.

The NAI also holds Inland Revenue registers of wills and administrations, 1828–39, containing abstracts of wills and administrations for 1828–1839 (indexed in separate volumes which cover the period 1828–1879; for the years 1840–1857) and Charitable Donations and Bequests will extract books containing abstracts of wills which made charitable bequests, 1800–1961 (there is a separate card index for the period 1800–1858 in the Reading Room). Grant books indexes in eight volumes for the years 1811–34 and 1835–58 (accession 999/611) are also available.

In addition, many thousands of copies of wills probated before 1858 have been collected over the years by both the NAI and PRONI. The NAI has indexed these in the main Testamentary Card Index in the Reading Room. A card index for pre-1858 surviving wills and will abstracts is also available in the Public Search Room at PRONI. This is arranged alphabetically by the name of the testator and provides the references to wills or extracts from wills that are scattered throughout PRONI collections. Altogether PRONI has over 13,000 copies and abstracts of pre-1858 wills.

There are manuscript indexes to the Consistorial and Prerogative Courts at the NAI. Some indexes have been published. The most important is the *Index to Prerogative Wills, 1536–1810* edited by Sir Arthur Vicars and published in 1897. This very important reference work for genealogists lists the full name, residence, title or occupation, and date of probate, for almost 40,000 names. It is a particularly important index for the Irish researcher because it serves as a guide to the names that can be found in *Betham's abstracts*. There are also genealogical pedigree charts available that were derived from

Betham's notes, and added to by many other persons, in the Irish Genealogical Office.

You can also consult the Eneclann CD-ROM, *Indexes to Irish Wills, 1484–1858* which can be purchased online at www.ancestry.com or at www.eneclann.ie. This CD-ROM contains over 70,000 entries from surviving wills, administrations, transcriptions and abstracts.

Wills 1858–1900

From 1858 district probate courts took over responsibility for wills and administrations from the Church of Ireland. The twelve probate registries created at the time were: the Principal Registry in Dublin and eleven district registries in Armagh, Ballina, Belfast, Cavan, Cork, Kilkenny, Limerick, Londonderry, Mullingar, Tuam and Waterford. The wills of wealthier members of society tended to be probated at the Principal Registry.

The district registries made transcripts of the wills that they proved and of the administrations intestate that they granted before the annual transfer of original records (20 or more years old) to the Public Record Office of Ireland in Dublin. The original wills were destroyed in Dublin in 1922 but the transcripts in will books survived. These are now on deposit in the NAI and PRONI, where they are available on microfilm for the period 1858–1900 (MIC/15C). Each volume contains an alphabetical index.

Will calendars

There is no comprehensive index to these post-1858 wills and grants. However, there are bound annual indexes called 'calendars' at both the NAI and PRONI. These calendars are of value to genealogists since they provide the name, address, occupation and date of death of the testator as well as the names, addresses and occupations of executors, the value of estate and the place and date of probate. Even if you have only an approximate date for the death of an ancestor it is worth looking through a number of volumes in the hope of spotting an entry giving details of their will.

When you are using these calendars to gain access to a will or transcript, the vital date to note is neither the date when the will was signed nor the date of death. It is the date of probate, i.e., the date when the will was officially proved in a probate registry. This date of probate is normally a few months after the person died. However, it is well to bear in mind that a significant number of wills were probated ten or more years after death. Such delays may have been more common where probate was in the Principal Registry in Dublin.

A consolidated index to the calendars for 1858–77 is available in the NAI and at PRONI. This gives the year and the registry where the will was probated. The Ulster Historical Foundation has an index to the calendars covering the period 1878–1900 on its website. This index gives the date of death and county of residence. Access to the index is available to members of the research co-operative, the Ulster Genealogical and Historical Guild.

PRONI also has a card index to post-1858 surviving wills and will abstracts. This index is most useful when you are looking for a copy or abstract of a will probate at the Principal Registry in Dublin, as the originals would have been destroyed in 1922 without a transcript being made.

Wills from 1900

The NAI holds original wills and administration papers lodged in the Principal Registry since 1904, and in most district registries, outside Northern Ireland, since 1900. PRONI has in its custody all wills for the districts of Belfast and Londonderry from 1900 to (at present) the mid-1990s, and for Armagh from 1900 until its district registry closed in 1921. Post-1900 original wills and their associated papers are available filed in a separate envelope for each testator. If an individual did not make a will there may be letters of administration that give the name, residence and occupation of the deceased as well as the name and address of the person or persons appointed to administer the estate. Post-1900 wills may be found by using the annual will calendars located in the reception area at PRONI.

An index to printed Irish will calendars 1878–1900, which includes surname and first name of testator, county or overseas country of residence and death, date of death and year of probate on around 151,000 individuals for all of Ireland, is available to members of the Ulster Genealogical and Historical Guild at www.ancestryireland.com.

7 Election Records

U NTIL THE EIGHTEENTH CENTURY elections were held infrequently. Before 1768 there was no law limiting the duration of Irish parliaments and nothing to compel the government to hold a general election except the death of the reigning monarch. The Octennial Act of 1768 provided that a general election should be held at least every eight years. Nevertheless, until the nineteenth century very few elections were contested, and parliamentary representation remained firmly in the hands of a small number of powerful landed families. The extension of the franchise changed this, and by the beginning of the twentieth century the landed classes had to a large extent withdrawn from electoral politics, particularly at representative level.

Qualifications for voting

Before the late nineteenth century the qualification for voting was generally linked to the tenure of land and only a small minority of men had the right to vote. In Ireland, between 1727 and 1793 only Protestants with a freehold worth at least 40 shillings per year had a vote. From 1793 to 1829 both Protestants and Roman Catholics with 40s freeholds had votes, although a Catholic was still unable to become a member of parliament. The 40s freehold was property worth 40s a year above the rent, and either owned outright or leased on certain specific terms. Many important and indeed prominent people had no vote because they leased their property on the wrong terms.

In 1828, Daniel O'Connell, who led the fight for Catholic Emancipation, won a by-election in Co. Clare. The fight for the right to sit in Parliament had gained unparalleled support throughout the country and resulted in the Catholic Relief Act of 1829. Catholics were now allowed to sit in Parliament and to hold government posts, except those of Lord Chancellor, Lord Lieutenant and Regent. However, at the same time as the Relief Act, the qualification for the vote was changed from 40s to £10. This reduced the electorate from 216,000 to 37,000.

The Reform Act of 1832, which although it retained the £10 franchise admitted certain categories of leaseholder, raised the county electorate to around 60,000. The Irish Franchise Act of 1850 set the county franchise at £12 with the result that the Irish electorate rose from 45,000 to 164,000. The majority of these county electors were farmers and were fairly well to do. As the century proceeded the right to vote was extended by a series of Acts in 1867 and 1884. By 1884 the majority of male householders over 21 were entitled to vote.

Women did not obtain the vote in general elections until 1918 and even then it was limited to those over 30 who were householders or the wives of householders. It was as late as 1928 that the vote was granted to women over 21.

Freemen records

The technical meaning of the term 'freeman' was a person who possessed the 'freedom' of a city or borough. The freeman had the right to vote in elections as well as exemption from certain fees. A person who held the freedom of a city did not necessarily live in the city. The members of the city and borough trade guilds were freemen.

A freeman's register usually stated the freeman's name, the date of admittance, his occupation (the guild to which he belonged), and the means by which he was admitted (birth, marriage or apprenticeship). Mary Clark's chapter 'Sources for Irish Freemen', in *Aspects of Irish Genealogy: Proceedings of the 1st Irish Genealogical Congress*, edited by Evans and O'Dúill, provides an introduction to the subject as well as bibliographies of manuscript and printed sources.

Freemen's lists are often found in the corporation books of boroughs, which may still be in local custody or may have been deposited or microfilmed (see Chapter 18). Dublin's freemen lists extend from *c*1234 to 1918. An alphabetical list of the freemen of the city of Dublin, 1774–1824, is available at the (NLI ILB 84133 D2). An online database of freeholders, freemen and voters by county, city and borough, 1234–1978, is available at www.ireland.progenealogists.com/freeholdersdata.asp

The *Report on Fictitious Votes*, 3 volumes, 1837 (furnished to the Irish House of Commons), contains complete lists of the freemen of the corporate town in all counties, the owners of rent-charges on estates in every county, also the returns of owners of houses in the towns of Armagh, Bandon, Coleraine, Dungannon, Galway, Lisburn, Londonderry, Newry and Youghal. Rights of freemen of the various trade guilds are set out, especially in cases of Dublin citizens, with many extract records showing the rights by descent from father to son, by marriage, etc. (see LDS film 1696697, items 8–11).

Freehold registers

One distinctive feature of the county franchise in Ireland was that from 1728 onwards voters had to conform to an increasingly tight system of registration, designed to prevent the creation of fictitious freeholders. This was important because the more 40s freeholders a landlord had on his land, the greater his influence during an election. Registers of freeholders list the names, addresses of individuals entitled to vote at parliamentary elections. Only by being registered to vote could a freeholder exercise his electoral rights.

During these periods of changes in the franchise, lists of those entitled to vote often appeared in the local newspapers. These lists are divided by barony and include voters' names and the townland in which they were resident. However, it is important to remember that those entitled to vote formed only a small percentage of the local population.

Poll books

Poll books are books in which are recorded the votes cast at parliamentary elections. They contain the name and address of the voter and often the address of the 'freehold' which entitled the voter to his vote. These records pre-date 1868, the year of the last election before Gladstone's Ballot Act 1872 established secret voting. This Act enabled tenant farmers to register their votes without having to take account of the political views of their landlord. Voters Lists and Freeholders Registers give similar information to the Poll Books but do not record how people voted at a particular election.

Electoral registers and voters lists

The Parliamentary Reform Act of 1832 required the publication on a parish basis of lists of persons eligible to vote. As the franchise has been gradually extended, so the lists have become more comprehensive. Since 1928 (when the age at which women were allowed to vote was lowered to 21) they have listed the names and addresses of all adults who have registered. Copies may be seen at county record offices and public libraries. PRONI, the NLI and NAI have extensive collections of electoral registers, although these are in no sense complete. Post-1880 voters' lists are to be found in the Crown and Peace Records for the counties.

Earlier records are scattered throughout various archives. Many can be found in the Landed Estate Collections. PRONI has recently digitized c. 5,500 sheets from pre-1840 registers and poll books. These can be searched online and images of the original records viewed. See www.proni.gov.uk/freeholders/intro.asp.

8 Boards of Guardians Records

THE NEW ENGLISH SYSTEM of poor law administration was applied to Ireland in 1838. Destitute poor who had previously been granted relief at parish level were to be accommodated in new workhouses, where conditions were to be as unpleasant as was consistent with health.

Ireland was divided into 137 poor law unions. These ignored traditional divisions, such as the county, barony and parish, and were centred on a market town where a workhouse was built. The boards of guardians were instructed to discourage all but the neediest paupers from applying to the workhouse from assistance. In their *Sixth Annual Report*, the Poor Law Commissioners admitted that it was no easy task to make conditions in the workhouse sufficiently bleak to deter only the most destitute:

> *It must be obvious to anyone conversant with the habits and mode of living of the Irish people that to establish a dietary in the workhouse inferior to the ordinary diet of the poor classes would be difficult, if not, in many cases, impossible; and hence it has been contended that the workhouse system of relief is inapplicable to Ireland.*

They were forced to rely on the 'regularity, order, strict enforcement of cleanliness, constant occupation, the preservation of decency and decorum, and exclusion of all the irregular habits and tempting excitements of life' to deter only the most desperate from seeking refuge within the workhouse.

The shadow of the workhouse loomed over most members of the working class and even some of the middle class. Orphaned families and foundling children, as well as women with large families who were suddenly widowed, were probably the most common inmates. Delicate children, or those suffering from epilepsy or disabilities, were also likely to end up in the workhouse, particularly during economic downturn or famine.

Life in the workhouse

It was a fundamental rule of the workhouse system that 'no individual capable to exertion must ever be permitted to be idle in a workhouse and to allow none who are capable of employment to be idle at any time'. The men were employed breaking stones, grinding corn, working on the land attached to the workhouse or at other manual work about the house; the women did house duties, mending clothes, washing, attending the children and the sick, as well as manual work including breaking stones.

The average day in the workhouse started at 7 am, when the inmates had to rise, dress in their workhouse clothes and then attend the central dining hall, where they waited for prayers to be read. The roll was called and they were inspected for cleanliness. They then lined up for their stirabout and milk. After breakfast the inmates were allocated work until late in the afternoon, when they had dinner of either potatoes or brown bread and soup. Inmates could not go to the dormitories until bedtime at 8 pm.

Even their leisure time was strictly monitored. They were not allowed to play cards or any game of chance, smoke or drink any 'spirituous or fermented drink'. They could see visitors only when accompanied by the master, matron or other duly authorised officer.

The novelist William Makepeace Thackeray visited the North Dublin workhouse in 1843. He later recalled:

Among the men there are very few able-bodied, most of them, the Keeper said, having gone out for the harvest time or as soon as the potatoes came in. The old men were assembled in considerable numbers in the long dayroom. Some of them were packing oakum by way of employment, but most of them were past work, all such inmates of the workhouse as are able-bodied being occupied on the premises. The old women's room was crowded with, I should think, at least four hundred old ladies, sitting demurely on benches, doing nothing for the most part. There was a separate room for the able-bodied females; and the place was full of stout, red-checked, bouncing women. If the old ladies looked respectable, I cannot say the young ones were particularly good-looking – silky, leering and hideous.

Who managed workhouses?

The management of the workhouses was the responsibility of boards of guardians composed of elected representatives of the rate-payers in each union, together with *ex officio* members including Justices of the Peace. While the guardians were legally responsible for the management of the workhouse and the collection and expenditure of money, the day-to-day running of the workhouse was carried out by a number of salaried officials. The clerk and treasurer of the Union operated the administrative system of the Poor Law. In terms of the management of the workhouse, the most important figure was the Master. He was also responsible for keeping records, such as the Master's journal.

The Great Famine

The poor law system was barely in operation before the catastrophe of the Great Famine hit Ireland. In the middle of September 1845 the maturing potato crop began to rot over much of the country. Throughout Ireland these workhouses in operation began to fill up for the first time since they had opened their doors. Fever, as usual, followed in the wake of the famine and relief committees were empowered to provide temporary hospitals, to ventilate and cleanse cabins and to procure the proper burial of the dead. By 1847 almost every person admitted into workhouses was suffering from either dysentery, fever or were in the early stages of disease. Under such circumstances separation became impossible. Disease spread and the whole workhouse became one large infirmary. During the first four months of 1847, more than 150 of the workhouse officers were attacked with disease, of whom 54 died, including seven clerks, nine masters, seven medical officers and six chaplains.

The workhouses nevertheless proved for many their only chance of survival. In their Annual Report of May 1848, the Irish Poor Law Commissioners underlined the importance of the workhouses in preventing a greater number of deaths during the Famine years: 'Including the large number of inmates maintained in the workhouses, we may state that more than 800,000 persons are daily relieved at the charge of the poor-rates, consisting chiefly of the most helpless part of the most indigent classes in Ireland; and we cannot doubt that of this number a very large proportion are by this means, and this means alone, daily preserved from death through want of food'.

Emigration

The alternative to starvation or death from fever in the workhouse was emigration. The Poor Relief Acts of 1838, 1843, 1847 and 1849 empowered the boards of guardians to raise sums 'not exceeding the proceeds of one shilling in the pound' from the annual poor rate to 'assist poor persons who would otherwise have to be accommodated in the workhouse' to emigrate, preferably to the British colonies. The Colonial Land and Emigration Commission was set up in England in 1840, under the control of the British Colonial Office, to organise and supervise emigration from both Britain and Ireland.

The boards of guardians agreed that assisted emigration should be organized for inmates who had no means of providing support for themselves, such as single mothers with young children, or female orphans whose parents had abandoned them in the workhouse. This was largely an extension of an existing policy, as workhouses in Ulster had for a number of years been arranging for inmates, both adults and children, to emigrate. A letter from Edward Senior, assistant poor law inspector, received by Newry, Kilkeel and other Ulster workhouses in April 1849 encouraged boards of guardians 'to send as emigrants to Canada any of the able-bodied inmates, especially females . . . in this move some of the permanent dead weight in the workhouse may be got rid of at a cost of about £5 or one year's cost of maintenance'.

New roles and responsibilities

The poor law system worked best between the 1850s and 1870s when the numbers receiving outdoor relief were small compared with those provided for in the workhouse. During that period the function of the workhouse gradually changed. It became an institution for the old, sick and vagrants.

During the later part of the nineteenth century the boards of guardians played an important role in the administration of local government. In 1872, they came under the control of the local government board, which became one of the most important departments of the Irish administration. To the boards of governors' original functions of supervising the poor law and the dispensary system, the government added many others including responsibility for public health.

From 1856 boards of guardians had acted as burial boards and from 1865 as sewer authorities for those areas of the counties which were outside the responsibility of the town commissioners. The guardians' powers were further increased by the Public Health Acts of 1874 and 1878, which made the boards rural sanitary authorities, giving them power to destroy unsound food, supervise slaughter-houses and deal with infectious diseases in hospitals. The guardians later were made responsible for the supervision of the hospitals set up under the Tuberculosis Prevention (Ireland) Act of 1908 and the boards also became the central authority under the Old Age Pensions Act of 1908.

The records

The poor law unions kept a number of different types of records. The NAI lists fifteen classes:

◆ Minute books
◆ Correspondence
◆ Accounts
◆ Statistics
◆ Out-relief

- ◆ Workhouse administration
- ◆ Workhouse inmates
- ◆ Workhouse infirmary
- ◆ Boarding out
- ◆ Dispensary
- ◆ Returns of births and deaths
- ◆ Vaccination
- ◆ Contagious diseases
- ◆ Assessment
- ◆ Miscellaneous

These are divided into subclasses, and even this classification does not cover every type of record one might possibly find.

Of all the records, the registers of admission and discharge are the most valuable. Unfortunately, the registers have not survived as well as other poor law union records. Of all the classes, the minute books are probably the best survivors. They contain miscellaneous information about the administration of the poor law unions, and often include details of staff employed by the poor law union.

Their location

The county libraries of Cavan, Donegal, Galway, Kerry, Kildare, Kilkenny, Laois, Leitrim, Louth, Meath, Offaly, Sligo, and the Tipperary joint libraries all have poor law union records, in particular, board of guardians' minute books. Addresses, and in some cases further details, will be found in the *Directory of Irish Archives*. The county council archives of Mayo, Roscommon, Waterford and Wicklow also hold poor law union records.

Other archives which have poor law union records are:

- ◆ Monaghan County Museum, which holds the records of Castleblayney workhouse;
- ◆ Limerick Regional Archives, which holds records for Counties Clare, Limerick and Tipperary;

◆ Cork Archives Institute;

◆ The de Valera Library and Museum in Ennis, Co. Clare, which holds poor law union records relating to County Clare.

The NAI also has a good collection, which contains a large quantity of Co. Dublin poor law union material. They have the minutes of the boards of guardians for the North and South Dublin Unions extending from 1840 to 1920. In 1920 the two unions were merged and the records of the united unions are available to 1938. The registers of admissions and discharges from these workhouses are available from 1940 to 1920.

The NAI also has similar records for the Rathdown Union, which covered parts of north Co. Wicklow and south Co. Dublin for the period 1839 to 1955. Records, mainly board of guardians' minute books, for Balrothery Union, Co. Dublin; Bawnboy Union, Co. Cavan; and Lismore Union, Co. Waterford are also held.

The NLI holds the board of guardians' minute books for the Mayo unions of Ballina, Ballinrobe, Belmullet, Castlebar, Claremorris, Killala, Newport, Swinford and Westport. It also has a number of miscellaneous items such as a letter-book for Ennistymon Union and accounts for some of the above-mentioned Mayo unions.

The archive departments of local authorities in the Irish Republic also hold extensive collections of poor law records, although the survival rate varies considerably.

The 27 poor law unions in the counties of Northern Ireland are held by PRONI as follows:

◆ BG1 – Antrim, Co. Antrim
◆ BG2 – Armagh, Co. Armagh
◆ BG3 – Ballycastle, Co. Antrim
◆ BG4 – Ballymena, Co. Antrim
◆ BG5 – Ballymoney, Co. Antrim
◆ BG6 – Banbridge, Co. Down
◆ BG7 – Belfast, Co. Antrim and Co. Down
◆ BG8 – Castlederg, Co. Tyrone
◆ BG9 – Clogher, Co. Tyrone

- BG10 – Coleraine, Co. Londonderry
- BG11 – Cookstown, Co. Tyrone
- BG12 – Downpatrick, Co. Down
- BG13 – Dungannon, Co. Tyrone
- BG14 – Enniskillen, Co. Fermanagh
- BG15 – Irvinestown, Co. Fermanagh
- BG16 – Kilkeel, Co. Down
- BG17 – Larne, Co. Antrim
- BG18 – [Newton] Limavady, Co. Londonderry
- BG19 – Lisburn, Co. Antrim
- BG20 – Lisnaskea, Co. Fermanagh
- BG21 – Londonderry, Co. Londonderry
- BG22 – Lurgan, Co. Armagh
- BG23 – Magherafelt, Co. Londonderry
- BG24 – Newry, Co. Down
- BG25 – Newtownards, Co. Down
- BG26 – Omagh, Co. Tyrone
- BG27 – Strabane, Co. Tyrone
- BG28 – Gortin, Co. Tyrone (united to Omagh *c.*1870)

For details of the records which have survived for each union, researchers should consult the grey calendars, which are available on the shelves of the Public Search Room.

School Records

I N THE EARLY YEARS of the nineteenth century there were numerous schools in Ireland but the general standard was low and many were badly conducted. Charter schools, established by royal charter in 1733 for the education of the poor, received grants from the Irish parliament and were built by private subscription. There was a great deal of Catholic opposition to these schools because of their proselytizing character. In May 1773, John Wesley, on a preaching tour of Ireland, visited Castlebar. He recalled the sight of the local charter school, which had no gate to its courtyard, a large hole in the wall, heaps of rubbish before its door and generally presented 'a picture of slothfulness, nastiness and desolation'. The next day he saw the children going to church unaccompanied by master or mistress. All were 'completely dirty'.

Many landlords took an interest in education. Lord Lurgan, for example, established Lurgan Free School on his estate in 1783, which provided education for the children of tenants regardless of religion. Mr and Mrs Hall, who toured Ireland shortly before the Great Famine, commented:

> *The principal proprietor of Tandragee is Lord Manderville, who, with his neighbours, Lords Farnham and Roden, Colonel Blacker and the Marquis of Downshire, have contributed largely to the present cheering condition of the County of Armagh. Lord Manderville has established no fewer than sixteen district schools on his estate in this neighbourhood, for the support of which he devotes £1,000 per annum, out of an income which is by no means large.*

There were also a large number of pay or hedge schools for Catholic children. These were usually set up by itinerant schoolmasters, who were paid according to the size of the school. Pay or hedge schools were sometimes, as their name suggests, held in the open air, but more commonly they were established in a local barn or cabin.

The Kildare Place Society, or to give it its proper name, the Society for the Education of the Poor in Ireland, was founded in 1811 and aimed to provide a system of interdenominational education. According to the 1824 report of a commission of inquiry into the state of public education, out of 56,201 children educated in the Kildare Place schools, 26,237 were Protestants and 29,964 Catholics. The Society originated as a voluntary institution but was soon after government funded. By 1830 the number of schools had risen to 1,634, but that same year the parliamentary grant was withdrawn and the number of schools quickly declined.

State-run schools

The establishment of a state-run system of elementary education did not take place until 1831, under the direction of the Chief Secretary, E.G. Stanley. The national schools which resulted were built with the aid of the Commissioners of National Education and local trustees. The curriculum was to be secular in content, though provision was made for separate religious instruction at special stated times. The National Board of Education assisted local committees in building schools and made a major contribution towards the teacher's salaries. A teacher-training school was established in Dublin. Model schools were set up gradually throughout the country.

The main criticism of the new system came from the Churches. The Established Church, the Church of Ireland, remained suspicious of these attempts to remove their influence over the education system. Ironically, the Roman Catholic clergy remained suspicious of what they continued to see as a proselytizing organization.

Mr and Mrs Hall, who remembered the old school-houses as 'for the most part, wretched hovels, in which the boys and girls mixed indiscriminately', were impressed by the transformation brought about by the Board of Education.

The school-houses, instead of being dark, close, dirty and unwholesome, are neat and commodious buildings, well-ventilated and in all respects healthful.

They were also impressed by the books supplied by the Board. These included an English grammar, arithmetic books for various classes, books on geometry and book-keeping, *An Introduction to the Art of Reading* and *A Treatise on Mensuration*.

Practical skills

As well as receiving an education, girls were taught needlework and the National Education Board encouraged the teaching of agriculture and gardening to boys and girls. The priorities of the Commissioners of National Education are indicated in a set of instructions given to inspectors in 1836:

> *He [the inspector] will ascertain the advancement of education among the children, noting the proportion of children who can read fluently; what progress they have made in writing and arithmetic; whether any be taught geography, grammar, book-keeping and mensuration; whether girls be taught sewing or knitting.*

School attendance

The number of pupils grew from 107,000 in 1833 to over half a million by the end of the century. Nevertheless, it is worth remembering that although Acts of 1876 and 1880 prohibited the employment of children under 10 years old and children up to 13 were required to attend school, the *Reports of the Commission for Education* make it clear that many children made only infrequent attendance at school. In his general report on the Armagh Circuit in 1903 Mr Murphy commented that:

> *The character of the attendance remains practically unchanged. The same causes are at work in town and in country and the same unsatisfactory results are noticeable. In rural districts the pupils attend for the most part very irregularly. This is due to the demand for child labour, and partly to a seeming inability on the part of parents to appreciate the injustice they do to their children, when they keep them from school without sufficient reason.*

The records

Unfortunately, few school records have survived from the eighteenth and early nineteenth century. PRONI holds records for the Southwell Charity School, Downpatrick, 1722–1970 (D/2961) and for the Thomas Jamison Charity School, Annahilt, 1839–1901, (D/3603). A good example of an estate school can be found in the records for Lurgan Free School, established in the 1780s for the education of poor children from all denominations in Shankill parish, which have survived in the Brownlow estate archive (D/1928/S). More details of early school records can be found in PRONI's *Guide to Educational Records*.

The records produced by the national school system can be divided into two sections: those made centrally by the National Board of Education and those which were made on a local level by the individual schools. The former are split between the NAI and PRONI. When the records were divided, some classes could not be easily split into those relevant to Northern Ireland and those relevant to the 26 counties. For this reason, some classes of documents which cover Northern Ireland, such as the teachers' salary books, remain in the NAI.

School registers

Between 1832 and 1870 something in the region of 2500 national schools were established in Ulster and the records that have survived for schools in Antrim, Armagh, Down, Fermanagh, Londonderry and Tyrone are held in PRONI. Of particular interest to the family historian are the registers of some 1500 national and public elementary schools (reference SCH). These registers generally date from the 1860s and they record information about each pupil: their full name; date of birth (or age on entry); religion; occupation of father and address of parents; details of attendance and academic progress; and the name of the school previously attended. A space is also provided in the registers for general comments, which might tell you where the children went to work afterwards or if they emigrated. Some registers have an index at the front which can greatly ease searching.

In many ways the information contained in the registers for this period can compensate for the lack of census records in the nineteenth century. PRONI has published a *Guide to Educational Records*, which includes an alphabetical list of all the schools for which it holds records. This is available on the shelves of the Public Search Room. Further information on using the school register collection at PRONI will be found in an article by Trevor Parkhill in *Familia* vol. 2, no. 1 (1985).

For those tracing ancestors in areas now part of the Republic of Ireland, things are considerably more complex. The vast majority of school registers remain in the custody of local schools or churches. Parish priests also hold some national school registers. Few have lodged their records in the NAI. Those that have include schools in Celbridge, Co. Kildare, Corlespratten, Co. Cavan and Glenaniff, Co. Leitrim. Some collections of correspondence relating to national schools have also found their way into the NAI. These include Ballyeaston, Co. Antrim; Ardrahan, Co. Galway, and Clonvaraghan, Co. Down. The registers of Denmark Street National School, Dublin, are available in the NAI on microfilm.

The most important accession of national school records the NAI has made recently was from the Representative Church Body. It consists of the records of sixteen national schools, sent there along with various collections of Church of Ireland parochial records. Ten of them have registers which start before the turn of the century. These are Drung and Maghera in Co. Cavan, Robertson's Parochial National School (Civil Parish of Raphoe) in Co. Donegal, St Stephen's (Civil Parish of St Peter) in Dublin City, Tuam Mall in Co. Galway, Cahirciveen in Co. Kerry, Rathmore in Co. Longford, Banagher in Queen's County, Drumbawn in Co. Tipperary and Inch in Co. Wexford.

You can view the lists for roll books and registers, lists for which are arranged by county; at www.nationalarchives.ie/topics/Nat_Schools/natschs.html.

Salary books

Salary books (NAI, ED4) are of particular interest to researchers with ancestors who worked in the national school system – there are over 1700 salary books for the period 1834–1918. Teachers are listed under their schools and details of their salary, rank and other miscellaneous career details are given.

From 1834 to 1844 each volume covers the entire country. From 1844 to 1855 volumes are arranged by county and after that by district. Within these volumes, the arrangement is numerical by school roll. The school roll number may be obtained in the card index in the NAI Reading Room. Unfortunately, there is no personal name index so it is usually necessary to know the school, or at least the area, a teacher taught in before attempting to find records of his/her career.

In addition to giving details of salary, salary books give the exact title of the job, for example, drawing master, medical attendant, or principal. Comments about the teacher's career are abundant; details of transfers, retirement or emigration are common.

Salary books for the model schools (ED5) contain the same kind of information as ED4.

10 Migration

THE IRISH WERE BY FAR THE MOST IMPORTANT MIGRANT group in Britain during the nineteenth century. They made their way to London and to all of the growing industrial towns of the Midlands, the north of England, and the central lowlands of Scotland. Victorian writers associated them with poverty, crime, drunkenness and Catholicism, which helped create the stereotype of the stage Irishman. However, many prospered in their adoptive country and some, like Richard Brindley Sheridan, Oliver Goldsmith, Edmund Burke and George Bernard Shaw, scaled the heights of English society.

London was a favourite destination for Irish settlers from the sixteenth century. According to contemporary sources there was a colony of Irish sailors and merchants by the Thames, Irish lawyers at the Inns of Court, and writers and dramatists in Whitefriars and Alsatia by the beginning of the seventeenth century. In St Giles especially there was a colony of 'unskilled labourers, builders' labourers, chairmen, porters, coal-heavers, milk-sellers and street hawkers, publicans and lodging-house keepers, apparently chiefly catering for their own countrymen'.

The emergence of the northern towns as great commercial and industrial centres during the eighteenth century encouraged the influx of Irish settlers. The Irish also flocked to Britain during the harvesting period, following the harvests round – haymaking in June, turnip-hoeing in July, corn-harvesting in August, hop-picking or fruit-picking in September. Politician William Cobbett described these seasonal workers as 'squalid creatures . . . with rags hardly sufficient to hide the nakedness of their bodies'.

The Great Famine

During the late 1840's the potato crop failed over the whole of Ireland, and that failure was repeated in successive years. Many starving and destitute people fled to the industrial towns on the British mainland. Liverpool was the first city to be invaded. At the beginning of 1847 *The Times* warned that 'the anticipated invasion of Irish pauperism had commenced, 15,000 have already, within the last three months, landed in Liverpool and block up her thoroughfare with masses of misery'. By June, it was estimated that 300,000 destitute Irish people had landed in the town. *The Times* predicted that 'in a few years more a Celtic Irishman will be as rare in Connemara as is the Red Indian on the shores of Manhattan'.

The Great Famine had a dramatic impact on the numbers migrating to Britain. By 1852, 22% of Liverpool's population and 13% of Manchester's was Irish-born. The largest settlement occurred in London, which according to the 1851 census was home to 108,548 Irish-born settlers. Today, more than 150 years after the Famine, the districts settled at that time are still identified as Irish: Hammersmith, Camden Town, Paddington and Islington.

A diverse community

In spite of their rural background the vast majority of Irish migrants settled in towns. In both 1851 and 1861 at least 31 towns in England and Wales had a recorded Irish-born population of over 1000. Some of these towns are not normally associated with an Irish presence – Bath, Colchester, Derby, Newport, Plymouth, Portsmouth and Southampton.

The poverty of many migrants' backgrounds and the fact that they were usually confined to the poorest neighbourhoods and lowest paid jobs made them an easy target for attack. 'Paddy' and his female equivalent 'Biddy' were depicted as poor, dirty, stupid and drunken. *Punch* drew the Irish with ape-like features and declared that:

A creature manifestly between the gorilla and the negro is to be met with in some of the lowest districts of London and Liverpool . . . It belongs in fact to a tribe of Irish savages . . . When conversing with its kind it talks a sort of gibberish. It is, moreover, a climbing animal, and may sometimes be seen ascending a ladder laden with a hod of bricks.

The Irish who came to Britain were a diverse group. A significant minority of them were middle class and blended more easily into British society. In cities such as Bristol there was no Irish quarter. The Irish were well distributed throughout the city and spanned the whole range of social groups. In Liverpool, although Exchange, Vauxhall and Scotland wards were recognized as Irish districts they rarely contained more than 50% of Irish population. Differences within the Irish community need also to be recognized. There was no single Irish identity among the Irish population. Within Irish communities, their fellow countrymen looked down upon both Connaught men and Orangemen from Ulster and religious differences were a frequent source of conflict between Irishmen in Britain.

The flow of migrants from Ireland continued for much of the twentieth century. From the First World War, Britain has replaced the United States as their first-choice destination, a position that it holds to the present day. Irish migration to Britain surged during the Second World War and after. As the Irish economy stagnated and British industry expanded, about half a million people left the Irish Republic during the 1950s alone. Today more Irish people live in London than anywhere else in the world except Dublin and Belfast. The Irish in Britain have never become a distinct and unified community, yet neither have they been fully integrated into British life. They still occupy, in the words of T.P. O'Connor during the First World War, a 'curious middle place'.

Records in Britain

Census returns

A census was taken in Britain every ten years after 1801 (except during the Second World War). Until 1841 the census was basically a headcount of the numbers of people (male and female), houses and families in a parish or township. From 1841 the census lists the names of everyone in the house, the address, approximate ages and occupations.

In 1841 those born in Ireland are recorded simply with the initial 'I' after their names. Later censuses are little better: entries for place of birth often simply state 'Ireland', although the name of a county or large town is sometimes given. In Scotland, from 1851, the specific town or parish of birth is given. Gravestone inscriptions and death notices in newspapers will probably provide the best means of identifying a more precise Irish address of an ancestor.

The original census returns for the 1841–91 or England, Wales, the Channel Islands and the Isle of Man are kept in the Family Records Centre in London. However, those for your particular county should also be available in the local record office. The 1901 census for England and Wales is available online at www.1901census.nationalarch ives.gov.uk/.

The 1851, 1861, 1871, 1881 and 1891 census returns hosted by www.ancestry.co.uk can be searched for free. For a fee images of the returns can be downloaded.

In Scotland there has been a census every ten years since 1801 (excluding 1941) but only those returns after 1841 (with a few earlier exceptions) carry details of named residents. Census returns for 1841–1901 can be consulted at the General Register Office in Edinburgh. Copies on microfilm may be consulted in LDS Family History Centres around the world. LDS centres also carry microfiche indexes to the 1881 census returns. Computerized indexes for the 1861, 1871, 1881, 1891 and 1901 censuses are available at the General Register Office in Edinburgh, and also online (for a fee) at www.scotl andspeople.gov.uk (includes images of the 1861, 1871, 1891 and 1901 censuses, and full transcript of 1881).

Wills

The Prerogative Court of Canterbury may have proved the wills of Irish people, usually the wealthier sort, who died with goods in England before 1858. These are held by the National Archives, London. Digital images of the wills are available online – it is possible to search for the will and download it for a small fee. See http://nationalarchives.go.uk/documentsonline/wills/asp. After 1858 wills would have been proved centrally at the Principal Probate Registry. Searches can be made there: indexes covering the period to 1943 are also on microfiche at many archives and Mormon FHCs.

In Scotland it was more common for people to make testaments, dealing solely with moveable goods. These were proved by local commissary courts under the Principal Commissariot of Edinburgh. From 1824 testaments were proved in county sheriffs' courts. All documents, 1513–1901. are viewable at www.scotlandspeople.gov uk, and can be downloaded for a fee.

Servicemen

Of course, many Irishmen served in the British Army and the Navy, and these records can be explored at the National Archives, London (see Chapter 15).

Births, marriages and deaths

Civil registration of births, marriages and deaths began in England and Wales in 1837 and in Scotland in 1855. These can be consulted at county record offices. The Family Records Centre (part of the National Archives) holds the union indexes of births, marriages and deaths registered officially in England and Wales from 1 July 1837. These are called union indexes because registration districts took their name from the poor law union in which they were based. You can search the indexes online for a small fee at www.findmypast.com.

The indexes to Scottish registers of births, marriages and deaths since 1 January 1855 and of births and marriages in the Church of Scotland from about 1553 are held at the Scottish General Register Office. There is also a computerized link to these records at the Family Records Centre in London, or you can search online at www.scotlan dspeople.gov.uk and view indexes of birth registrations (1855–1906), marriages (1855–1931) and deaths (1855–1956), again for a small fee.

Those wishing to trace baptismal or marriage records from before July 1837 should consult the *International Genealogical Index*, known as the IGI. This is an index to births, baptisms and marriages worldwide, although coverage is not complete. The indexes to the British Isles cover the period from the beginning of registration to 1875. The indexes for England and Wales are mainly to Church of England parish registers and to nearly all the registers in RG4 in the National Archives.

Family Records Centre

The Family Records Centre (FRC), run jointly by the General Register Office and the National Archives, London, provides direct access to some of the most important family history research in England and Wales, including births, marriage and death records, census returns and wills. The returns for all census years have now been fully indexed by name and linked to digitized images, available at www.nationalarchi ves.gov.uk/census, which can be accessed free of charge in the Online Resources Area.

The FRC also holds microfilm copies of Prerogative Court of Canterbury wills and administrations, and associated indexes, covering the period 1383–1858. The National Archives Documents Online website www.nationalarchives.gov.uk/documentsonline provides online access to the whole collection. More detailed information on the FRC can be found at www.familyrecords.gov.uk/frc/.

The FRC will soon be moved to the National Archives building at Kew.

For more detailed information on the records available in England, Scotland and Wales, you should consult two other titles from How To Books: *Tracking Down Your Ancestors* and *Meet Your Ancestors*.

Emigration

FOR MUCH OF ITS HISTORY, Ireland had been a country of emigration. It is estimated that half of all the people born there since 1820 have emigrated and that more than 70 million people world-wide are of Irish origin. From the Great Famine of 1845–7 to the 1950s, the natural increase in the population was continually offset by out-migration on a scale which was relatively higher than for any other European country, leading to an almost continuous decline in the population for more than a century.

It is important that researchers living abroad should exhaust the material available at home before furthering their investigations in Ireland. Check old diaries and letters; note relevant dates recorded in family Bibles and seek information from relatives both at home and in Ireland. It is also important to find out what is available in local archival institutions.

Research in the United States

The history of emigration to America is dominated by the mass exodus during the period of the Great Famine and its aftermath, when more than a million people fled Ireland for North America. In Ulster, where the effects of the Great Famine were less dramatic than in the South and West of Ireland, emigration reached its greatest peak during the eighteenth century. These emigrants were for the most part Protestant, and in particular, Presbyterian.

Passenger lists

The USA has comprehensive passenger lists for ships arriving from 1820, but they provide only two clues relating to the origin of the emigrant – the port of departure of the ship and the nationality of the passenger. This is of limited value when it is realized that the vast majority of Irish emigrants in the nineteenth century sailed from Liverpool. It was not until 1893 and the Immigration Act that the former address in Ireland of an emigrant was recorded.

Many passenger lists have been published in books and on CD-ROM or on the Internet. Many of these can be found at the library of the Society of Genealogists, and at PRONI, NAI and NLI. *The Famine Immigrants: Irish Immigrants arriving at the Port of New York, 1846–1851*, by I.A. Glazier and M. Tepper, contains an impressive 650,000 names. B. Mitchell has produced a number of books, including *Irish Passenger Lists, 1803–06. Lists of Passengers Sailing from Ireland to America Extracted from the Hardwick Papers* (GPC, 1995) and *Irish Passenger Lists, 1847–71, Lists of Passengers Sailing from Londonderry to America on Ships of the J&J Cooke Line & the McCorkell Line* (GPC, 1988).

An invaluable website containing a number of lists is run by the American Immigrant Ship Transcription Guild (www.istg.rootsweb.com). Perhaps the best overall guide to passenger ships between Ireland and the United States is www.genealogybranches.com/irishpassengerlists.

Also check the American Family History Immigration History Centre Ellis Island website, an online database of 22 million passengers and crew members who went through Ellis Island (New York), for the period 1892 to 1924: www.ellisislandrecords.org.

The websites www.ancestry.com and www.genealogy.com also have indexes listing millions of Irish immigrants to America.

Census records

A census has been taken every ten years in the USA since 1790, and from 1850 the returns provide the country of birth and age of all members of the household, not just the head of household. Sometimes the census enumerator has recorded more specific information than just the country of birth. Those before 1930 are searchable online at www.ancestry.com (with 1880 free at www.familysearch.org).

Many state censuses also exist. These were generally taken between federal censuses and contain information similar to that found in the federal censuses.

Birth, death and marriage certificates

These may help to pinpoint your immigrant ancestor's origins if he or she married or died in the United States. Although the quality of information held on death certificates varies according to where they were filed, they may give the exact birth date, the age in years and the birthplace, which may be the townland, city, parish, county or just 'Ireland'.

If your Irish ancestor married in the United States, the marriage certificate might identify where the bride and/or groom was born in Ireland and perhaps even their ages. Parents' names are often listed. Birth, marriage and death certificates of children may also help identify where their parents where born.

The United States has no national registry of births, marriages and deaths. Such records are held locally by either the county or state. The best sources are www.cyndislist.com under the individual state, and A. Eakle and J. Cerny, *The Source: a Guidebook of American Genealogy* (Ancestry, new edn. 1996 by L. Szucs and S. Luebking). Some civil registration is becoming available at www.ancestry.com. You can also write to the appropriate government office to order a copy of a birth, marriage or death certificate. The US Department of Health and Human Services publishes a list of current addresses and fees in a booklet entitled *Where to Write for Vital Records*. You can also search birth, marriage and death indexes for many states on www.ancestry.com.

Military records

Irish immigrants have fought in many wars since the American War of Independence. Army records are a valuable source for family history. Military service records, pension applications and draft registration cards are just some of the most valuable records available.

For those with ancestors who fought for the colonial forces, the *DAR Patriot Index*, compiled by the National Society Daughters of the American Revolution, contains information on both men and women who fought between 1774 and 1783. The index generally provides birth and death data for each individual, as well as information on spouse, rank, area of service, and the state where the patriot lived or served. The National Society Daughters of the American Revolution provides a free online service at www.dar.org/natsociety/pi_lookup.cfm.

Military service records have also been abstracted from the National Archives group 93, and published in four volumes (Waynesboro, TN: National Historical Publishing Co., 1995). The abstracts include the soldier's name, unit and rank. A similar index is available online to subscribers at www.ancestry.com.

The *American Genealogical-Biographical Index* includes the names of people who have appeared in more than 800 published volumes of family histories and other genealogical works. These include several volumes of published Revolutionary War records, such as *Historical Register of Virginians in the Revolution, Soldiers, Sailors, 1775–1783* and *Muster and Payrolls of the Revolutionary War, 1775–1783* from the collection of the New York Historical Society.

Pierce's Register was originally produced by the government in 1915 and published by the Genealogical Publishing Company in 1973. It provides an index to Revolutionary War claim records, including the veteran's name, certificate number, military unit and the amount of the claim.

For a more complete listing of available records and databases see genealogy.about.com/od/revolution/index.htm?terms=pension+ser vices.

Civil War pensions

Civil War soldiers, their widows and heirs filed claims for military pensions. Those for Union veterans are held by the National Archives, Washington. These claims include many details of family members, often providing birth and marriage information. The name of the county or townland of the veteran's birth is also often specified.

The National Archives, Washington, does not have pension files for Confederate soldiers. Pensions were granted to Confederate veterans and their widows and minor children by the States of Alabama, Arkansas, Florida, Georgia, Kentucky, Louisiana, Mississippi, Missouri, North Carolina, Oklahoma, South Carolina, Tennessee, Texas, and Virginia. These records are in the state archives or equivalent agency.

First World War registration cards

Draft registration cards for Americans involved in the First World War (1917–18) list details, including date and place of birth (and father's birthplace), for about 24 million men born between 1872 and 1900. These cards are searchable by name on www.ancestry.com, with digital images available for all cards.

Research in Canada

Irish emigrants, particularly those from Ulster, have set up home in every Canadian province and played an influential role in national life. A considerable number of letters deposited at PRONI relating to the period 1815–45 are from emigrants writing from Canada. This is not necessarily confirmation, however, that the authors settled in Canada. Many Ulster people migrated to the United States via Canada. It was cheaper to travel to Quebec from the port of Londonderry than to go from Belfast or Liverpool to Boston or New York. The voyage was also usually shorter.

The first large-scale settlement of Upper Canada came when Loyalists – many of them Scots-Irish – fled from the United States during the American War of Independence. A second wave of immigration, coming directly from Ulster, consisted of disbanded soldiers and small farmers hit by the agricultural slump which followed the Napoleonic Wars. Canadian territory in the post-Napoleonic War era was attractive in that there was less competition for it than for land on the eastern seaboard of the United States. One visitor to Canada in the early part of the nineteenth century commented:

> *. . . from the number of Irish and Scotch who have found their way into Canada by a detour through the States, for few or none have come direct, and from the satisfaction they express with their situation and prospects, one might be led to consider this country as the natural receptacle for our superabundant population. But the northern Irish only, chiefly from the counties of Down, Antrim, Londonderry, Tyrone and Donegal, have as yet, settled in the province . . .*

Census records

The earliest major census of Canada was taken in 1666 in the area which later became Quebec. The names, ages and occupations of all men, women and children were recorded parish by parish. Of particular interest are the censuses taken after 1851, which name the entire household, with age, occupation, birthplace, religion, martial status, gender, race and other details listed for each person. Hundreds of districts of the 1901 census have been indexed and are searchable on www.ancestry.com.

The Church of the Latter Day Saints (Mormons) have indexed the 1881 Canadian census. This index contains 4.3 million names and may be searched online at www.familysearch.org.

Library and Archives Canada has posted digital images of the 1901 and 1911 censuses on the Canadian Genealogy Centre website at www.genealgy.gc.ca. The Ontario Genealogical Society has also published a head-of-household index to the 1871 returns for Ontario.

Passenger lists

In 1895, after it was noted that 40% of all passengers arriving in Canada were actually bound for the USA, a system of joint inspection of immigrants coming 'overland' from Canada was established. From 1847, the two ports of Portland and Falmouth, Maine were becoming increasingly popular as ports of entry for Irish immigrants coming down from Quebec and the Maritime Provinces to the USA. In these cases, therefore, Irish immigrants leaving Canada for the USA will be noted.

Few passenger lists survive for vessels arriving in Canada before 1865. The Family History Library has microfilms of surviving passenger lists for Quebec, 1865–1900, and Halifax, 1881–1899.

Birth, death and marriage records

In the absence of passenger lists the best hope of linking an ancestor to their place of origin in Ireland may lie in the identification of a marriage entry for a newly arrived immigrant in a church register. Frequently, the marriage registers give the county of birth in Ireland, and occasionally, the exact place of origin of bride and groom. In the years 1801 to 1845, for example, the weddings of 3000 Irish immigrants, with parents' names and native parishes, were recorded in Halifax, Nova Scotia.

Civil Registration in Canada started at different times in each individual province as follows: Novia Scotia, 1864; Ontario, 1869; British Columbia, 1872; Saskatchewan, 1878; Manitoba, 1882; New Brunswick, 1888; Newfoundland, 1891; Alberta, 1897; Prince Edward Island, 1906; Yukon and Northwest Territories, 1896; and Quebec, 1926.

Records are held by the provincial Registrars General and, apart from Quebec, access is usually only by application – see www.cyndislist.com under each province. www.ancestry.com now has some Ontario and British Columbia Civil Registration online.

Land grants

Land grants can be extremely useful in identifying recent immigrants. To obtain land from the colonial government and, after 1867 from the provincial authorities, a settler had to make a formal application, known as a petition, in which details on place of origin, date of arrival in Canada, names of wife and children and their ages are often given. There is a computerized *Land Records Index* for the years 1780 to 1914 with two alphabetical listings, one by applicant's name and one by township.

Researching in Australia

Emigration to Australia did not get going in a major way until the 1820s, after the disruption of the Napoleonic Wars. The distance involved, and the logistics of the journey, meant that the numbers going to Australia as compared with North America were much smaller. For the same reasons emigration to Australia was much more controlled. Regulation was applied at points of departure in Britain and Ireland and at entry points in Australia.

There were also government-assisted schemes such as the emigration of workhouse inmates to Australia. Labour had become extremely scarce in Australia around the time of the Great Famine in Ireland and the colonists in New South Wales and Western Australia pressed the Colonial Office to secure more settlers. Arrangements were made with the Colonial Land and Emigration Commissioners for a scheme of assisted emigration and the first 5000 adults were sent in 1847.

Those emigrants who arranged their travel to Australia were generally better off than those who left Ireland for North America. The costs involved in shipping out to Australia were obviously much higher. Australia, therefore, attracted a significant proportion of emigrants with the resources to set themselves up in business or on the land in the expanding agricultural hinterland of the coastal settlements.

Australia has a superb collection of records for the genealogically minded. The three prime sources of convict records, assisted immigration lists, and birth, marriage and death certificates provide a wealth of relevant detail for those tracking down their Irish ancestors. Convict indents, in which the convicts were listed by ship on their arrival in Sydney, date from 1788, i.e., from the earliest beginnings of the colony. The early indents give the name, date and place of conviction for every convict, while those from the 1820s also provide their native place and age. This detail on individual convicts can also be followed up in Ireland in local newspapers or at PRONI in the Crown and Peace Archive.

Census records

A number of census records from the nineteenth century were lost in a major fire, and none from the twentieth century have been retained, apparently for reasons of protection of privacy, and a fear that failure to protect privacy would put the accuracy of the census in doubt. Early census records have survived for each of the states as follows:

New South Wales: Records date back to the original convict 'return' of 1788, which was essentially the earliest Australian census, including people on Norfolk Island. There are censuses from 1828, 1841 (available online at www.records.nsw.gov.au/), 1891 and 1901 (the latter was destroyed, but in both cases collectors' notebooks have survived).

South Australia: South Australia was part of New South Wales until 1836, which means records before that come under New South Wales. The census of 1841 has survived, and can be seen online at www.jaunay.com/1841.census.html, with all the names listed at www.jaunay.com.census.html.

Tasmania: Tasmania (its original name was Van Diemen's Land) was part of New South Wales until 1825, and so most early records come under that. Many musters, the earliest from 1803, have been published, and you can find the complete census records up to 1857 at the Archives Office of Tasmania (www.archives.tas.gov.au/).

Victoria: It was only in 1851 that Victoria separated from New South Wales. This means that many records before this come under New South Wales. However, you can find convict returns for 1825 and 1828, after which there are four separate census returns going to 1844, all of which can be seen in the Public Records Office of Victoria (www.prov.vic.gov.au/).

Western Australia: The first Western Australia record is the 1829 Swan River muster, after which you can find the returns from four censuses, the last of which was taken in 1859. Records are in either the State Archives (www.sro.wa.gov.au/) or the Battye Library (www.liswa.wa.gov.au/battye.html).

Northern Territories: The Northern Territories were part of South Australia from 1863 to 1911, after which they became a Commonwealth Territory. The censuses of 1881 and 1891 are available in the National Archives (www.naa.gov.au/).

Passenger lists

Passenger lists document the movement of people into and out of Australia. The master of each passenger vessel and aircraft arriving in, or departing from, Australian ports was required to provide the authorities with a list of passengers disembarking and embarking from that port. Depending on the port, passenger lists and crew records are deposited at the state capitals: Hobart, Sydney, Canberra, and Perth. Passenger lists are publicly available once they are more than 30 years old.

The National Archives are responsible for records of the Commonwealth government of Australia. The Commonwealth government assumed responsibility for passenger arrivals and departures in 1923, so its holdings date mostly from 1924, although it does hold some records dating back to the 1850s. Unfortunately, there are no comprehensive name indexes for passenger records. To search for family members effectively, it is necessary to know the year, month and the port or state where they landed. Passengers were listed under each ship so knowing the ship's name is also useful when searching these records. If you are unable to identify the date of arrival within two months, your search could be very time-consuming.

Transportation records

The transportation of convicts to Australia came about as a result of the British government's problems coping with an eighteenth-century crime wave at home that threatened to overwhelm the inadequate prison system. Defeat by the colonists during the American War of Independence had resulted in the loss of the convict settlements of North America so the government turned to the new territories in Australia. Between 1791 and 1853 about 40,000 to 50,000 convicts were transported from Ireland to Australia. A number of Irish records on convicts have been microfilmed and indexed by name and can be searched at www.nationalarchives.ie/topics/transportation/search01.html.

Births, deaths and marriages

These records are an invaluable source of information on the origins of Irish Australians. The Genealogical Society of Utah has published a CD-ROM collection entitled *Australian Vital Records Index, 1788–1905*, which indexes 4.8 million births, marriages and deaths in a number of locations. It may be purchased online at www.familyseach.org.

Researchers can search the civil registration of New South Wales online at www.bdm.nsw.gov.au for births, 1788–1905; deaths, 1788–1945; and marriages, 1788–1945.

Australasian Genealogical Computer Index

The Australasian Genealogical Computer Index is a microfiche collection of approximately two million records of cemetery transcriptions, newspaper articles, Irish transportation records and other material. It is available at the Family History Library and at a number of libraries in Australia.

Researching in New Zealand

The two main islands of New Zealand are situated more than 1000 miles to the east of Australia. British interest in New Zealand began when Captain James Cook circumnavigated both islands on the *Endeavour* in 1796:

'We saw in the bay several canoes, people upon the shore and some houses in the country,' he wrote in his journal. 'The land on the seacoast is high with white steep cliffs, and inland are very high mountains. The face of the country is of a hilly surface and appears to be clothed with wood and verdure.'

New Zealand came under the jurisdiction of New South Wales until it became a Crown colony in 1840. Many early settlers came into New Zealand by way of New South Wales, so Australian records should be consulted if you are attempting to trace early settler ancestors.

An article in the October 1845 edition of the *Dublin University Magazine* noted that New Zealand was 'the most recent, remotest, and least civilized of our colonies'. In subsequent years it noted:

> *We cannot omit a brief examination of the main attractive features of New Zealand as a place of residence for Englishmen. Favoured with a climate that shames that of Australia, and with a soil exuberant in the highest degree, presenting also many alluring young settlements with vast and fertile plains on their skirts, those islands are every year more largely engaging the attention of emigrants.*

It was not until the arrival of fencible soldiers and their families who settled at Penmure, Howick, Onehunga and Otahuhu in Auckland between 1847–1852 that New Zealand received a substantial influx of Irish settlers. Pensioned from the British army these settlers were eager to escape the Great Famine in Ireland and the industrial strife in Britain. They were offered free passage for themselves and their families with guaranteed work, a two-room cottage and an area of land, provided they attended church parade and up to 12 days of training per year.

In the 1860s the South Island's population rose from 50,000 to 159,000 as Australian diggers swarmed across the Tasman in the gold rushes. By 1873 no fewer than 46 New Zealand emigration agents were operating in Ireland. The New Zealand government was particularly anxious to encourage single women to emigrate, as the Minister of Immigration explained in 1883:

> *Of the [1,941] Irish, 1,124 are single women; and the Government have not deemed it desirable to exclude any of these, by endeavouring to maintain the proportions as strictly as was originally contemplated.*

Passenger lists

Passenger lists in New Zealand, as in Australia, were kept at the port of arrival. Most official passenger lists are in the National Archives in Wellington but many other lists are held locally. The earliest are those for the New Zealand Company vessels, arriving at the ports of Wellington, Nelson, New Plymouth and Otago. These lists date from

1840 and provide the immigrant's name, age, occupation, wife's age and children's age and sex. From 1853, provincial governments at Canterbury, Wellington, Nelson, Auckland and Otago administered New Zealand. Each province compiled passenger lists of varying quality. The arrival of ships and passengers was reported in local newspapers and these are worth consulting for detailed accounts of the immigrants and their voyages.

Census records

The first full census in New Zealand was conducted in 1851, and the census was triennial until 1881, at which time it became five-yearly. Unfortunately, in both New Zealand and Australia census records were destroyed once the relevant statistical information had been extracted from them.

Births, deaths and marriages

Civil registration of births and deaths began in 1848, but marriages were not recorded until 1855. In terms of identifying the Irish origins of an ancestor, death certificates are an extremely valuable source, especially after 1876. From that year the place of birth, the parents' names and the date and place of marriage of the deceased were recorded. Marriage certificates from 1880 are equally useful as they give the birthplace and parents' names of both bride and groom.

Access to all birth registers held at the New Zealand National Archives is restricted, but death and marriage registers held can be accessed. The complete registers of births, deaths and marriages are held by the Central Registry of Births, Deaths and Marriages, Department of Internal Affairs, www.bdm.govt.nz.

Parish records

Parish registers of baptisms, marriages and burials, held either by local clergy or, in the case of Presbyterian records, in their archives in Dunedin. These should be consulted for details on births, marriages and deaths before the commencement of civil registration. Most gravestones have been transcribed and are on microfilm at branches of the NZSoG.

Research in Britain

By 1851, thanks to the impact of the Great Famine, there were over 727,000 Irish-born persons living in Britain. For many Britain was the first step in their plans to earn enough money to pay for a passage to America.

Emigration records held at the Public Record Office, London

◆ *Board of Trade Outwards Passenger Lists, 1890 to 1960* (BT 27) are lists of passengers leaving the United Kingdom by sea, arranged by date and port of departure. The name, age, occupation and place of residence of each passenger are given. Lists earlier than 1890 no longer exist.

◆ *Registers of Passenger Lists, 1906 to 1951* are held in BT 32. Before 1920 they give, under the different ports, the names of ships and the month of arrival and departure. After 1920 the exact date of arrival and departure is recorded. Before 1908 the registers relate only to the ports of Southampton, Bristol and Weymouth.

◆ *Privy Council Registers, 1540 to 1978* (PC 2) contain numerous entries about the colonies as well as petitions and letters of people going there or already resident there. Also worth consulting is the *Calendar of Acts of the Privy Council of England, Colonial Series, 1613 to 1783.*

◆ *Audit Office Declared Accounts, 1779 to 1827* (AO 1) include references to the pensions and allowances paid to emigrants, American loyalists and others in the colonies, as do the *Declared and Passed Accounts, 1803 to 1848* (AO 2), which also give lists of establishments in some of the colonies. The *Various Accounts, 1539 to 1886* (AO 3) list the names of some individual settlers.

◆ *West Jersey Society Records, 1675 to 1921* (TS 12) relate to tracts of land in West and East Jersey, Pennsylvania, New England and elsewhere, divided up as shares of the company. The records contain many names in the original correspondence, minute books, registers of shares, original deeds, and papers about claims.

◆ *Ministry of Health Poor Law Union Papers, 1834 to 1890* (MH 12) include material about parish-assisted emigration under the New Poor Law of 1834, arranged alphabetically under county and union. Correspondence between the General Board of Health and the Colonial Land and Emigration Commissioners, 1853 to 1854, is in MH 13/252 and between the Poor Law Authorities and the Emigration Commissions, 1836 to 1876, in MH 19/22.

In the main, Colonial Office records concern those North American colonies which later became Canada. *Colonial Office: Emigration Original Correspondence, 1817 to 1851* (CO 384) includes letters from settlers, or prospective settlers; names appear in the *Entry Books, 1815 to 1833* (CO 385) and in the *Land and Emigration Commission papers, 1840 to 1876* (CO 386). Some volumes of *Colonies, General: Original Correspondence* (CO 323) and *Entry Books* (CO 324, 1662 to 1872; CO 381, 1835 to 1872) give details of land grants and applications.

It is also worth searching original correspondence for North America, together with its related registers, in the following record classes:

◆ CO 6 – British North America Original Correspondence, 1816 to 1868

◆ CO 326 – General Registers, 1633 to 1849

◆ CO 327 – British North America Emigration Registers, 1850 to 1863

◆ CO 328 – British North America General Registers (including emigration 1864 to 1868)

◆ CO 329 – British North America Registers of Out-letters, 1872 to 1880

Research in Ireland

It is not enough to know that your emigrant ancestor came from somewhere in Ireland. In order to use any of the major record collections deposited in Irish archives you must have some idea where in Ireland an ancestor came from, preferably a townland or parish location. It also makes the search a lot easier if you have some idea when your ancestor emigrated and the port at which he or she arrived. In many cases the family historian is dependent on family tradition for answers to these questions, but in most cases various records can be searched for information before a visit to Ireland.

The most obvious sources for researchers who are descendants of emigrants from Ireland are the emigration records deposited in PRONI or the NAI. Unfortunately emigration is not, as a general rule, particularly well documented. No official registers of passengers leaving Irish ports in the nineteenth century were kept except for a few copies of passenger lists for the period 1803–1806 which were among the papers of the Lord Lieutenant, the Earl of Hardwicke, now in the British Library. These have been published in the *Ulster Genealogical and Historical Guild* (vol. 1, 1978–84) complete with an index.

Public Record Office of Northern Ireland, Belfast

The following passenger lists are held by PRONI and relate largely to destinations in the USA:

◆ List of passengers from Warrenpoint and Newry to Philadelphia and New York, 1791–2, T /711/1

◆ Passenger lists – Philadelphia, 1800–82, MIC/333/1

◆ Passenger lists – Baltimore, 1890–92, MIC/333/2

◆ Passenger lists – Boston, 1871–91, MIC/333/3

◆ Passenger lists – New York, 1826–27, 1840–42 and 1850–52, MIC/333/4

◆ Passengers from various origins arriving mainly in New York, 1802–1814, T/1011

◆ Passenger lists from Belfast, Cork, Limerick, Londonderry, Newry, Sligo, Warrenpoint to USA, 1803–1806, T/3262

◆ Passenger lists from Ireland to America, 1804–1806 (index available in Deputy Keeper's Report 1929), T/521/1

◆ Passenger books of J&J Cooke, Shipping Agents – sailings from Londonderry to Philadelphia, Quebec, St John's, New Brunswick, 1847–71, D/2892/1/1-14 (see also MIC 13)

- List of names of petitioners for naturalization, Laurens County, South Carolina, 1806–1825, T/3538

- Typescript list of passengers to America from Co. Londonderry 1815–16, T/2964

- List of passengers and crew giving age and occupation of people emigrating from Belfast, Cork, Limerick, Londonderry, Newry, Sligo and Warrenpoint, 1805–1806, MIC/303

The Ordnance Survey compilers also recorded the names, ages, religion and townland addresses of emigrants for many parishes in Counties Antrim and Londonderry for a few years during the period 1833 to 1839. Again, Canada and the USA were the major destinations of these emigrants. These two sources have now been indexed and published by the Genealogical Publishing Company of Baltimore.

The following are of particular interest to researchers interested in emigration to Canada:

- Three volumes of passenger lists, February 1847–9, February 1850 to August 1857, March 1858 to July 1867, of J&J Cooke, shipping agents, Londonderry. The Canadian destinations are Quebec and St John, New Brunswick, with details also being given for Philadelphia and New Orleans. Reference D2892/1/1-3.

- Typed transcripts, compiled in 1984, of notices which appeared in Canadian local newspapers, mostly the *New Brunswick Courier*, 1830–46, and the *Toronto Irish Canadian*, 1869. The notices include queries as to the whereabouts of various persons who had emigrated from Ulster to Canada and the United States. Reference D/3000/82.

- Passenger list, 11 May 1847, issued by A.C. Buchanan, Chief Agent for Emigration at Quebec, giving the dates of sailing, the names of the ships involved, their point of departure and the numbers of passengers carried. Reference T/3168.

- For details of the early migration from Ulster to Australia see the Crown and Peace Presentment Books for Counties Antrim and Down, ANT2/2A/1 and DOW 2.

For emigration to Australia, the following records are of particular importance:

◆ Passenger list, 1840, Victoria, Australia, T3036

◆ Register of the Girls' Friendly Society, who sponsored emigrants from various counties in Ireland, 1890–1921, D648/9

◆ Indexes to births, deaths and marriages in New South Wales, Australia, 1787–1899, M.F.4

In all more than 4000 orphans were sent to Australia from workhouses in Ireland. The names of those selected from Ulster workhouses are given in the minute books of the boards of guardians. Further details of their background can be obtained by consulting the admission registers. See the records of the boards of guardians (BG).

A more unusual source is the files of the Tuberculosis Authority in the period just after the Second World War. This archive contains two files (1948–57) relating to the X-raying of emigrants who applied for the assisted-passage schemes that were on offer to the United States, Australia or New Zealand. Reference TBA 6/5/3-4.

There are many references to parishioners and members of congregations who emigrated to various parts of the world in church records. These most commonly occur in Presbyterian Church records owing to the long-standing association of that Church with emigration. The notations are often found in communion or communicants' rolls and include the date of the emigrants' departure and which members of the family left at that time. The circuit schedule books of Methodist churches record numbers of emigrants from their midst, and occasionally the emigrants are named.

The easiest way to locate emigration records is to use the computerized *Subject Index* which is located in the Reception Room (a print-out is available on the shelves of the Public Search Room). Under the subject heading 'Emigration', researchers will find a brief description of the records, the relevant dates and the appropriate reference number. Researchers should also consult the *Place Names Card-Index* in the Public Search Room, which contains numerous references to letters from settlers in America, Canada, Australia, New Zealand, etc.

The National Archives of Ireland

The NAI holds a wide range of records relating to transportation of convicts from Ireland to Australia covering the period 1788 to 1868. In some cases these include records of members of convicts' families transported as free settlers. To mark the Australian Bicentenary in 1988, the Taoiseach presented microfilms of the most important of these records to the government and people of Australia as a gift from the government and people of Ireland. A computerized index to the records was prepared with the help of IBM and is available for use at various locations in Australia.

This index to the transportation records can be found on the NAI website at www.nationalarchives.ie. It should be noted, however, that the records from which the transportation database was compiled – transportation registers and petitions to government for pardon or commutation of sentence – are incomplete. While the collection of convict petitions dates from the beginning of transportation from Ireland to Australia in 1791, all transportation registers compiled before 1836 were destroyed. Therefore, if the person you are researching was convicted before 1836, but was not the subject of a petition, he or she will not appear on this database.

12 Landed Estate Records

Estate records

U NTIL THE LATE NINETEENTH CENTURY Ireland was a country of large estates. Visitors to Ireland were struck by the great mansion houses like Powerscourt, Castletown and Castle Coole. Gate lodges, demesne walls and model villages, such as Adare, Celedon and Moy, are reminders of way in which the great estates dominated the countryside.

Many of the great estates were concentrated in easily identified territorial blocks, often comprising dozens of townlands. The greater estates were often distributed through two or three counties; the Marquis of Downshire had 115,000 acres in Antrim, Down, Kildare, King's County and Wicklow; Lord Landsdowne owned 120,000 acres in Counties Dublin, Kerry, Limerick, Meath and Queen's; and the Marquess of Conyngham owned more than 156,000 acres in Clare, Donegal and Meath.

Landowners

Many of these landowners were to play a major role in the economic development of the country, particularly in the areas of agriculture, linen production and the establishment of market towns. Local magistrates were recruited from the gentry; at general elections until 1880 they played an important role in returning members of parliament; they dominated county administration until 1848 and the poor law until the 1880s. The importance of the major landowners to the development of the surrounding countryside was acknowledged by Mr and Mrs Hall, who toured Ireland shortly before the Great Famine. They were struck by the fact that Ireland was, to a greater extent than Great Britain, a stratified society:

> In Ireland, as yet, the aristocracy of wealth has made little way, and to be of a 'good family' is a surer introduction to society than to be of a large fortune.

The Irish playwright Brendan Behan famously described the Anglo-Irish aristocracy as 'Protestants on a horse'. In fact, although greatly outnumbered by Protestants, there were many Catholic landlords in Ireland. The Duke of Leinster, Ireland's premier peer, and the Marquess of Ormonde were the heads, respectively, of two historic Anglo-Norman families, the Fitz Gerlands or Geraldines and their traditional rivals the Butlers. Lord Inchiguin was descended from the O'Brien High Kings and Arthur MacMorrough Kavanagh from the MacMorrough, Kings of Leinster. In Ulster, the Earl of Antrim and Lord O'Neill were both descended from ancient Celtic families.

From the mid-1870s the size of most estates could be found in *Thom's Directory*. This took the form of an alphabetical list of landowners of 10,000 acres and upwards and a list of landowners in Ireland of 1000 acres and upwards who owned land situated in different counties. By the 1870s over half the land was owned by fewer than 1000 major landlords. A list of the landowners was compiled in 1871–76 by government order and printed in the *Return of Owners of land of One Acre and Upwards, in the Several Counties, Counties of Cities, and Counties of Towns in Ireland, to which is added A Summary For Each Province and for All of Ireland (Presented to both Houses of Parliament by Command of Her Majesty)* (Dublin, 1876). Copies are available at major archives and libraries.

Tenant farmers

By the middle of the nineteenth century more than three quarters of the population lived in rural areas. Tenant farmers and their families accounted for half the rural population, numbering about 500,000 in the 1860s. As a group they were more varied than the landlords, their holdings ranging from a few acres to large graziers such as Edward Delany of Woodtown in County Meath. About 20 per cent had leases, but the majority of tenants were tenants at will, holding their land from year to year. The Ulster Custom in the North left the tenants in a much better position than those in the other provinces. It was a practice or usage by which a tenant paying rent to his landlord could not be evicted without being paid by the incoming tenant, or by the landlord, the full marketable price of his interest in the farm, this interest being the value of his own improvements, and those inherited from his ancestors. This custom ensured that the landlord could not raise the rent as the tenant effected improvements in his holding.

Agricultural labourers

The largest group found in the countryside was agricultural labourers. Most of these lived in one-room mud cabins. Furniture usually consisted of a bed of straw, a crude table and stool, and a few cooking utensils. Labourer and cottier shared a potato diet. Many labourers were casually employed and they could be thrown out of their cottages with only a few weeks' notice. They often moved from place to place in search of work. Although ostensibly employed on one of the great estates they generally worked for one of the tenants and therefore are not mentioned in the great estate collections; nor can they be picked up in the electoral registers because they did not have the vote until 1885.

The Great Famine

During the Great Famine many landlords, already burdened with debt and facing the crippling poor law payments with income badly affected by the non-payment of rents, were forced to sell their estates, often heavily mortgaged. During the 1850s more than 5 million acres, almost a quarter of the land in Ireland, passed into the hands of new landlords many of whom were wealthy speculators.

The impact of the Great Famine and agrarian and political unrest during the middle of the nineteenth century resulted in the break-up of the great estates as government-assisted schemes enabled tenants to buy the land from the local landlord. This culminated in the Irish Land Act of 1903 (better known as the Wyndam's Act), which offered the landlords an incentive to sell out their entire estates. The purchase terms were also made easier for the tenant with the repayment period being extended to 68½ years.

The records

Estate papers are an invaluable source for family historians. It is not uncommon to find that the records of a single estate have been deposited in more than one archival institution. The family may have donated the papers in their possession to one institution, while those retained by an estate office or solicitor may have been passed on to another. Nevertheless, estate papers offer the best opportunity to trace ancestors into the eighteenth and even seventeenth century. They include information not only on the great families who once dominated Irish society, but also on the army of servants, tenants, labourers, shopkeepers and craftsmen with which they came into contact. One of the main items of expenditure on many of the larger estates was servants' wages, for no Irish big house was complete without a large array of retainers, most drawn from the locality, details of which can be found in wage books and household accounts.

The quality of estate papers varies enormously from estate to estate but many include leases, rentals, deeds, maps and correspondence covering every aspect of life on the estate. As a general rule the records of the larger, better managed estates have tended to have a better survival rate than those of smaller concerns.

Tenants and leases

A landlord grants a lease to a tenant, who is given the right to occupy the property for a specific period of time. Two copies of the lease were usually prepared. The original lease was signed by the landlord and kept by the tenant. The counterpart was signed by the tenant and kept by the landlord. A lease was usually for a term of years, 1, 21, 50 or 99 years. The maximum term of a Roman Catholic lease was 31 years until the 1778 Act altered this.

In Ireland, as in the western half of England, leases were usually for three lives: the lease expired when all of the three persons named in the lease had died. The lease was stated to continue for 99 years or, if earlier, until the death of the last named person. In a lease for lives the names of relatives are often included. The lease could be renewed at the fall of each life by inserting a new name on payment of a renewal fine. The three-life lease was therefore in reality in perpetuity as long as the tenant wished to renew it. Three-life leases are very useful for genealogists because a tenant frequently named members of his family (particularly sons and grandsons) as the lives. When new lives were inserted details of age and relationship were often included and it is possible to work out when the old life died.

Tenants often sublet the property, or part of it, to a third party; this was known as a sublease. The third party became an undertenant, paying rent to the tenant, who continued to pay rent to the landlord. A subtenant may not be picked up in the records of the estate, and this can be frustrating when you know that an ancestor leased land in a particular area. It is therefore worthwhile examining the correspondence between a landlord and his agent because this can be of immense genealogical value. Not only does it include details of the day-to-day running of the estate, but also mention is often made of those who worked on the estate.

Estate ledgers contain records with particulars of rentals, long and short term leases, names of heirs in cases of leases for lives in two or three generations, assignments, and fines upon the fall of a life, the death being noted. There are frequently lists of tenants at will or of those who held leases of less than three years' duration. Full rent rolls, dated from time to time, contain the names of the tenants, names of the leased lands (townlands) or parts thereof held by each, the conditions of tenure, including valuation of the property, the length of each lease and provisions for renewal, the annual rent and fines due, and the amount of the paid or unpaid balance. Landlords or estate agents often kept tithe lists, voters' lists, seventeenth-century muster rolls, and notes concerning family alliances and the character of various tenants.

Rentals

Rentals allow local historians to trace individual tenants and over a period of time show how one plot of land or property changed hands. Records were generally arranged by year (rents were usually paid half-yearly) or with several years covered by the same volume. The information provided will usually be limited to the name of the tenant, the extent and location of his holding and the rent payable by him.

Occasionally rentals are annotated with a change in occupancy, and the reason for it is sometimes given. Title deeds, although more cumbersome to use, include any documents that have been used to prove ownership to the property.

Maps and plans

Maps and plans form an important element in most estate collections. These show the property of the landlord, who would have employed a surveyor to illustrate the extent of his land and the more important features on his estate. Maps come in all shapes and sizes and can be coloured or roughly sketched in black and white. Often there are blank spaces where the land does not belong to the surveyor's employer.

Surveys may include the names of tenants and the extent of their holdings. They give many place names that have long disappeared and show the location of vanished mills, woodland, paths and houses. They illustrate the method of agriculture employed in a particular area and the size of fields and holdings.

Evictions

A tenant could be evicted for non-payment of one year's rent or without cause by service of notice to quit at the termination of a yearly tenancy. Although evictions were sometimes carried out to facilitate the consolidation of holdings or the move over to pasture, most evictions were for the non-payment of rent. For most of the Victorian period evictions remained on a much smaller scale than the wholesale clearances during and immediately after the Great Famine. Evictions rose again during the agricultural depression of the late 1870s and the early 1880s. Evictions and debt collections were very public affairs and often made the local press.

Ejectment books contain a wealth of genealogical information: the names of hundreds of tenants, the location of the farms and sometimes details of the lease. Random evictions had occurred before the 1840s but it was the dreadful years of the Famine which witnessed thousands of evictions. Major Denis Mahon at Strokestown, Co. Roscommon evicted 3006 people in 1847 alone. In June 1849, 567 were evicted in one day from the Tipperary estate of the Reverend Massey Dawson. Captain Kennedy, the poor law inspector for Co. Clare witnessed that more than 22,000 who were evicted from the Kilrush area between 1847 and 1879:

> *These helpless creatures, not only unhoused but driven off the lands, no one remaining on the lands being allowed to lodge or harbour them. It is obvious they must go somewhere till disease and privation thin their numbers; and wherever they acquire a residence the proprietor must eventually suffer, both in purse and character for the neglect or cupidity of others.*

Ejectment Books can be found in estate collections held by the National Library and National Archives, Dublin, and the Public Record Office of Northern Ireland.

Finding estate records

For anyone who thinks that their ancestor may have been a tenant farmer on one of the many landed estates in Ireland, it is first of all necessary to identify which estate it may have been. The easiest way to identify the name of a landowner is to examine Griffith's Valuation of *c.*1860 for the relevant townland and note the name of the immediate lessor. For the names of landowners in the early nineteenth century the *Ordnance Survey Memoirs* of the 1830s can be consulted.

The Irish Manuscript Commission carried out a programme aimed at surveying all collections of estate papers in private hands whose owners were willing to have them examined. A report was written on each collection. Representative samples of these reports were published in *Analecta Hibernica*, nos 15, 20 and 25. The entire collection of reports is available for examination at the Genealogical Office, 2 Kildare Street, Dublin.

Each report consists of a number of foolscap-size typescript pages, bound in volumes. *Analecta Hibernica* no. 20 contains a names index keyed to the reports. A list of the reports made up to 1965 is given in *Analecta Hibernica* no. 23 and those made since that date are listed in *Analecta Hibernica* no. 32 (1985). If there is a report on the estate papers of the landlord you are researching his name will appear in one of the lists along with the number of the relevant report.

Where are estate records held?

Estate records are held by repositories throughout Ireland including PRONI, the NAI, NLI, Trinity College, Dublin, the Boole Library at NUI, Cork, the Hardiman Library at NUI, Galway, and the Cork Archives Institute. Some are deposited in local libraries and museums.

With many of the great landed families owning land on both sides of the Irish Sea, Irish estate records are also held in British archives. Indeed, in the case of absentee or semi-absentee landowners who had estates in Ireland and Britain, estate collections can be scattered amongst a number of repositories. This will require greater detective work on the part of the family historian, who will need to find out where the records have finally been deposited. Most county record offices in Britain publish summary guides to their holdings on the Internet and copies of the detailed reports and calendars are available centrally in the National Register of Archives at www.hmc.gov.uk/nra/indexes.htm.

Marriage and inheritance have ensured that many Irish estate papers remain in private hands and outside Ireland. Material relating to the properties of the O'Briens, Earls of Thomond, in Counties Carlow and Clare, for example, is held in Petworth House, West Sussex. Private owners in both Ireland and Britain vary in their willingness to allow access to their collections.

Reference books and directories

There are a number of works of reference available, particularly for the second half of the nineteenth century, which will enable the family historian to locate the relevant estate (at least on a county basis). The most important of these are John Bateman *The Great*

Landowners of Great Britain and Ireland (reprinted with an introduction by David Spring, Leicester, 1971) and U.H. Hussey De Burgh *The Landowners of Ireland: an Alphabetical List of the Owners of Estates of 500 Acres or £500 Valuation and Upwards in Ireland* (Dublin, 1881).

For the nineteenth century a variety of gazetteers and directories are available which offer some information on landowners in an area. The most useful gazetteer for pre-Famine Ireland is Samuel Lewis *A topographical dictionary for Ireland* (2 volumes, London, 1837). It is organized on a county basis and parishes within each county are in alphabetical order. Directories such as *Thom's*, *Slater's* or *Pigot's* also provide some information on estates. *Slater's*, for example, provides lists of the prominent nobility and gentry families in each area. There are also directories which deal with individual counties (see Chapter 16).

Genealogical information on landlords and their families can be found in works such as G.E. Corkayne *Complete Peerage of England, Scotland, Ireland etc., Extant, Extinct and Dormant* (revised edition by Vicary Gibbs and others, 13 volumes, London, 1910–49), Sir Bernard Burker Burke's *Landed Gentry of Ireland* (London, various editions) and Burke's *Peerage, Baronetage and Knightage* (London, various editions).

Richard J. Hayes's *Manuscript Sources for the History of Ireland Civilization* is one of the surest ways of locating estate records. For the family historian the most relevant volumes are numbers 1–4, dealing with persons, and 7–8, dealing with place. In these volumes the researcher should look up the name of the landlord or the name of the area(s) where the estate was located. Because landlords tended to have titles and unusual surnames, the problem of confusion over common surnames is not as serious as it is with tenants. Hayes gives the name of the repository in which the estate papers are stored and occasionally a brief list of the documents in the collection. Some repositories will supply a full list, from which one can order selected items.

Collections in provincial and national archives are also summarized in the excellent *Directory of Irish Archives* by Seamus Helferty and Raymond Refausse.

Records in the NLI

In the NLI, the card catalogue in the manuscript reading room should be consulted as these cards contain information on more recently acquired estate papers not to be found in Hayes's *Manuscript Sources*. There are also 'special lists' available on family or estate collections which have only recently been sorted. *Special List A* is an index to these collections. It records the number of the list in which a collection is catalogued and this list can be consulted in the manuscript reading room.

One should also consult the periodic reports of the Irish Manuscript Commission and NLI on estate collections in private hands, which are also available in the NLI. Among the more notable of these landed estate archives are: Castletown (Co. Laois), Clements (Counties Leitrim and Donegal), Clonbrock (Co. Galway), Coolattin (Co. Wicklow), De Vesci (Co. Laois), Doneraile (Co. Cork), Headfort (Co. Meath), Inchiquin (Co. Clare), Lismore (Co. Waterford), Monteagle (Co. Limerick), O'Hara (Co. Sligo), Ormond (Counties Tipperary and Kilkenny), Powerscourt (Co. Wicklow), Prior-Wandesforde (Co. Kilkenny), Sarsfield (Co. Cork), and Wicklow (Co. Wicklow).

Records in PRONI

Landed estate records form the bulk of privately deposited material in PRONI. In 1924 the first Deputy Keeper of the Records of Northern Ireland wrote to many of the Province's prominent families asking them to deposit their archives in PRONI. The 3rd Duke of Abercorn (Northern Ireland's first Governor) was the first to respond to this appeal, and the Abercorn Papers (recently purchased from the present Duke), constituting some 50,000 documents, are among the most important of PRONI's landed estate collections. The extent of these collections can be judged in PRONI's *Guide to Estate Collections*, published in 1994. The *Personal Names Index* in the Public Search Room can also be consulted under the landowner's name. Examples of some of the larger estate collections can found on PRONI's website at www.proni.gov.uk/records/landed.htm.

Other sources

The firm of solicitors that acted for the landlord may still be in business. They may know something about the location of the estate papers or may even have them in their possession. The easiest way of finding out the name of the firm that acted for the landlord is through the Land Commission. The bulk of Irish agricultural land was sold by the landlords, through the Land Commission, to their tenants between 1881 and 1923.

It is sometimes possible to contact the descendants of nineteenth-century landlords, and the modern-day representatives of the family may be able to give information on the location of estate papers. The various editions of *Burke's Landed Gentry of Ireland* and *Debrett's Peerage and Baronetage* can prove very useful in this regard. People with titles are particularly easy to trace forward using those books, as the addresses of the present-day title-holders are usually listed.

Local libraries, heritage centres and local archives are worth checking. They may have the records, or the personnel may know where to find them. Local historians may have located estate records in the course of their researches on related subjects. Historical journals usually give sufficient details about the authors of articles to enable readers to contact them.

Encumbered estates

The Great Famine had a massive impact on the management and economic viability of landed estates. Many estates were mortgaged and landowners unable to collect rents were forced to sell their estates. Some landlords had to sell parts of their estates to remain solvent. By an Act of Parliament in 1849 an Encumbered Estates Court was established with authority to sell estates on the application of the owner or encumbrancer (one who had a claim on the estate). After the sale the court distributed the money among the creditors and granted clear title to the new owners. The Landed Estates Court assumed the functions of this court in 1853. Between 1849 and 1857 over 3000 Irish estates were sold to approximately 3200 purchasers.

There are five sequences of rentals which have survived pertaining to these courts, two of which are found in the NLI, two in the NAI, and one in PRONI. The most complete sequence is that referred to as the O'Brien rentals stored in the NAI and consisting of almost 150 volumes. Indexes are available in the various repositories which guide researchers to the relevant landed estate if it was sold through the Encumbered Estates or Landed Estates Court.

These printed rentals or particulars of sale were issued before the sale of a property and therefore contain very detailed information on tenants and holdings on each estate in order to attract potential buyers. They are divided into counties, townlands and tenements, and include the names of the parties involved and the date, maps of the estate giving tenants' names and, on occasion, surveys of the estate. Many landlords owned properties in local towns and villages, and these too can be found in the Encumbered Estates Rentals. Before 1862, the maps were usually the work of valuators, but after that date they were official Ordnance Survey maps.

13 Taxation and Valuation Records

Tithe applotment books, 1823–38

THE TITHE WAS NOT A TAX but a charge upon land. The tithe system, which nominally earmarked one-tenth of the produce of the land for the maintenance of the clergy, was introduced in England as early as the eighth century. It was introduced in Ireland during the reign of Henry II, although it was not paid outside the area around Dublin until the reign of Elizabeth I.

In Ireland, because the tithe system was used for the upkeep of the Established Church (Church of Ireland) only, it caused a great deal of unrest among Roman Catholics and Dissenters including Presbyterians and Quakers. Very few of the eighteenth-century tithe records have survived. In 1823 the Tithe Applotment Act was passed, which stipulated that henceforth all tithes due to the Established Church were to be paid in money rather than in kind, as they previously could have been. Between 1823 and 1827 holdings in each civil parish were valued based on the average price of wheat and oats in the parish during the seven years preceding 1 November 1821. This necessitated a complete valuation of all tithable land in Ireland, the results of which are contained in the manuscript tithe applotment books for each civil parish.

Tithe applotment books

The tithe applotment books are unique records giving details of land occupation and valuations for individual holdings prior to the devastation brought about by the Great Famine and the resulting mass emigration. They list the occupiers of tithable land, not householders, as is the case in a census. Therefore, landless labourers and weavers were omitted, in addition to all purely urban dwellers. In 1838 the tithe payment was reduced by 25% and transferred from the tenant to the landowner. Tithes were finally abolished in Ireland in 1869. The names of the tithe payers are usually arranged alphabetically by townland and by parish and county. Unfortunately there are no accompanying maps to show land division on a field-by-field basis.

Using tithe books

The NAI holds manuscript books for almost every parish in the 26 counties of the Republic of Ireland (more than 2000 in total) giving the names of the occupiers, the amount of land held, and the sums to be paid in tithes. They are also available on microfilm at the NLI and the Gilbert Library in Dublin. More than 270 volumes were sent to PRONI for parishes in Counties Antrim, Armagh, Cavan, Down, Fermanagh, Londonderry and Tyrone.

The researcher can face problems in using the tithe books. In some areas, for example, the land was of such poor quality that no tithe could be levied. Other areas were tithe-free for other reasons, usually because the Church owned the land outright. Another, more serious complication is that the subsequent dividing-up and renaming of townlands, and the transfer of townlands from one parish to another and even from one county to another, is the cause of some confusion.

The *Householders' Index*, available on the shelves of the Public Search Room at PRONI and the NAI, can be used as a guide to the surnames listed in the tithe applotment books.

An index to the tithe applotment books is available on CD-ROM from Heritage World.

Tithe defaulters

With increasing numbers of tithe payers refusing to pay tithes during the years 1830 and 1831, in particular, many Church of Ireland clergymen found themselves in difficult financial circumstances. The government set up the Clergy Relief Fund 1831, so called because the clergy could claim for arrears for only that year. The government, rather than the clergymen, had the job of collecting the arrears of tithes in each parish.

If a clergyman wished to seek assistance under the terms of the Act which set up the Clergy Relief Fund, he had to swear an affidavit setting out the methods he had employed in attempting to recover the arrears of tithe for 1831. To accompany the affidavit he had to write out a schedule, 'hereunto annexed', setting out the 'Names, Descriptions, and Places of Abode of the Persons, Occupiers of Land' within his parish or the 'Representatives of such of them as are dead'. He also had to state how much tithe was due from each tithe payer and how much each tithe payer was in arrears. The affidavits and the schedules then had to be sent to Dublin Castle for a decision as to whether or not relief would be granted.

There are 1061 pages of names of tithe defaulters. These pages cover 232 parishes and list 29,027 names. This is a unique record of people living in Ireland, and of their address and occupation, at the time that the various schedules were compiled in June, July and August 1832. The records are held in the NAI in what are called the *Official Papers Miscellaneous Assorted* files.

Valuation records

The levying of a rate in Ireland, to raise money to meet the costs of local government, dates from 1635. An Act of that year gave Justices of the Peace power to levy certain sums, known as the county cess or grand jury cess, upon the inhabitants of a local area for the execution of public works such as roads and bridges. By 1824, Parliament recognized the need for a more equitable method of measuring liability for cess and rates. The 1st Valuation Act was introduced in 1826 and a valuation of the whole of Ireland was prepared.

The townland valuation of the 1830s

Though often dismissed as being of fairly limited genealogical value, the townland valuation carried out in the 1830s can be an important source for those searching for their ancestors, particularly if those ancestors were urban dwellers. The records consist of manuscript field books (more than 4500) compiled by parish, and describe each townland in the parish; the quality of the aril, and its valuations. Although the townland valuation was primarily concerned with the agricultural value of land, it also included details on houses valued at £3 or over (in 1838 this was raised to £5 or over but by this time most of Ulster had been surveyed). In the rural areas the names of only a few householders are given, and these tend to be of the gentry or the better class of tenant farmer. In towns, however, many more houses were substantial enough to reach the valuation, with the result that a large number of householders are recorded.

A set of field books for most parishes in Northern Ireland (except for Co. Tyrone) and for the Republic is available in the NAI under the reference OL5. Those for Northern Ireland are available at PRONI under the reference VAL/1B; the accompanying annotated maps are listed under VAL/1A and VAL/1D.

Unfortunately, major towns and villages are not listed separately, but under the parish and barony in which they are located. In order to find the appropriate volume it is necessary to identify the parish. This can be done by consulting the *Alphabetical Index to the Townlands and Towns, Parishes and Baronies of Ireland*, which is available on the shelves of the Public Search Room at PRONI and the NAI. It is simply a matter of locating the relevant town and then running a finger along the columns listing the barony, parish, and poor law union.

The first general valuation (Griffith), 1848–64

The 1848–64 valuation gives a complete list of occupiers of land, tenements and houses. This Primary Valuation of Ireland, better known as Griffith's Valuation, was to determine the amount of tax, or rates, each person should pay towards the support of the poor and destitute within each poor law union. The value of all privately held lands and buildings in both rural and urban areas was determined according to the rate at which each property could be rented year after year. The tax was fixed at about 6% (with variations), for every pound of the rent value. Griffith's Valuation is arranged by county, within counties by poor law union division, and within unions by parish. It includes the following information: the name of the townland; the name of the householder or leaseholder; the name of the person from whom the property was leased; a description of the property; its acreage; and finally the valuation of the land and buildings.

The published version of Griffith's Valuation was based on the valuers' notebooks. It did not, however, include all the information provided by the notebooks, and some entries in a later published version have been updated. Earlier surveys were not included. PRONI has, for example, 59 manuscript volumes containing the valuation of Antrim, 1939; Cavan, 1841, and Down, 1839. A valuation of the City of Armagh was published in 1839. It contains the name and annual value of every holding in the city. A copy is available at the Irish Studies Library, Armagh and the NLI. County and city libraries will normally hold those volumes relating to their localities.

Griffith's Valuation is of particular interest to anyone wishing to trace their family tree, because so little of the nineteenth-century census returns has survived. It is especially important for identifying emigrants' precise place of origin during this period. Emigration statistics point to the fact that a large proportion of the mass emigration that took place as result of the Great Famine of 1845–51 did not occur until after 1855, by which time the valuation was largely complete for the south and west of the country.

Family historians should be aware that Griffith's Valuation has some limitations. Partnership farms held under the rundale system had their individual parcels bracketed together without being separately measured, thereby excluding certain tenant names.

Where to find records from Griffith's Valuation

The NAI holds the original Valuation surveyors' notebooks for the 26 counties of the Republic of Ireland. Those for parts of Co. Carlow, and for the Unions of Abbeyleix and Birr, Co. Tipperary, are missing. The notebooks consist of 'field books', 'house books' and 'tenure books'. All of these record a map reference for the holdings to which they relate. Of particular interest to the family historian are the house books, which record the occupier's name and the measurements of any buildings on their holdings. The tenure books give details of the annual rent paid and the year of any lease, which can be useful when searching estate papers of the Registry of Deeds.

The original notebooks for Northern Ireland are available at PRONI, reference VAL/2B. The valuers' annotated set of Ordnance Survey maps showing the location of every property is also available at PRONI (VAL/2A).

Printed editions of Griffith's Valuation are available in the public search rooms of the NAI and PRONI and at major libraries throughout Ireland. These volumes are arranged by poor law union, within union by county, and then subdivided into parishes and townlands. There is an index at the front of each volume which enables searchers to identify the page or pages in which a specific townland may be found.

An index to Griffith's Valuation for all of Ireland is available on CD-ROM from Heritage World in Donaghmore. A CD-ROM set comprising page scans of the printed Griffith's Valuation has also been produced by Irish Microfilms Media Ltd in Dublin.

A unique archive

The Valuation Office at the Irish Life Centre, Abbey Street Lower, Dublin 1, established to administer Griffith's Valuation in the 1850s, holds a list of occupiers of property for the 26 counties in the Republic of Ireland going back to 1846. The following details are held in relation to each property:

◆ occupier name,

◆ townland,

◆ address,

◆ description of property,

◆ acreage of holding,

◆ rateable value,

◆ reference to the property's position on a valuation map.

The archive is unique in that it can relate people to a particular property. In addition, the property location is outlined on a valuation map. The valuation maps are also archived so it may be possible to locate the exact position of a house or property of a particular family back to *c.*1850.

Valuation revisions

Another set of useful records are the 'cancelled land books' and 'current land books', which give details of all changes in the holdings from the time of Griffith's Valuation to the present day. When a change of occupancy occurred, the name of the lessee or householder was crossed off and the new owner's name written above it, while the year was noted on the right-hand side of the page. This helps to establish significant dates in family history, such as dates of death, sale or emigration. By the closing years of the nineteenth century most of the occupiers of land had become landowners, thanks to a series of Land Purchase Acts. This explains the initials L.A.P. (Land Act Purchase) that may be found stamped on an entry in the revision lists.

These volumes are arranged by poor law union within counties, and then subdivided into parishes and townlands. There is an index at the front of each volume which enables searchers to identify the page or pages in which a specific townland may be found. The *Householders' Index* can be used as a guide to the surnames listed in Griffith's Valuation.

The Valuation Office at the Irish Life Centre, Abbey Street Lower, Dublin 1, holds the cancelled land books for the Republic of Ireland. PRONI holds those for Northern Ireland, reference VAL/12B. The corresponding maps are also available at PRONI, reference VAL/ 12D.

Based on the findings of Griffith's Valuation is *Landowners in Ireland: Return of Owners of Land of One Acre and Upwards*, which records more than 32,000 owners of land in Ireland in 1876, identifying them by province and county. It is available on the shelves of the Public Search Room at PRONI, the NAI and at major libraries.

Irish Land Commission

The Land Commission was set up in 1881 under the Land Act of that year. Its main function became the advancement of money to tenants to enable them to purchase their holdings and the fixing of fair rents under the various Land Acts from 1881 onwards. Because the Commission had to be satisfied that potential purchasers would be able to repay their annuities it employed inspectors to assess the capacity of tenants to make their repayments. Therefore, the Land Commission records are one of the few sources which reveal as much about the tenants as about landlords.

Deposited records of the (now defunct) Irish Land Commission date from the seventeenth century onwards, but are not yet catalogued or generally available for public inspection. The records, contained in some 50,000 boxes, were amassed as a result of the operation of the Irish Land Purchase Acts 1881–1923. Records include deeds dating from the seventeenth century, tenants' purchase agreements and resale maps and other records created under the auspices of the numerous administrative branches of the Land Commission.

The best existing search aid was compiled by the NLI, entitled *Records in the Irish Land Commission: Survey and Guide*, and takes the form of typescript volumes and card indexes (accessible only in the NLI). An index to the wills and administrations (which simply gives the name and address and the date of grant of probate or letters of administration) is available on the shelves in the Public Search Room in PRONI. By writing to the Keeper of Records, Land Commission, Bishop Street, Dublin 8, you may be allowed to examine the schedules of areas and accompanying maps but without special permission you cannot access the remaining material.

The records of the Irish Land Commission concerning sales of estates in Northern Ireland to tenants were transferred from Dublin to Belfast in 1922 and were subsequently deposited in the Land Registry archive (ref LR/1) at PRONI. The Land Registry archive, which contains an estimated 50,000 items, is one of the largest held in PRONI and contains numerous classes of records which will be of interest to genealogists. Title deeds, for example, relate to the tenure of property, including its origin, length of lease and other conditions under which the lease was held. Title deeds often include papers from the eighteenth and early nineteenth centuries which recite names of people formerly associated with the property. Testamentary papers include wills and other testamentary material which should prove to be useful to research of a genealogical nature.

There are three indexes which can be used to identify documents likely to be of interest to researchers:

◆ alphabetical index by name of estate,

◆ numerical index by record number,

◆ numerical index by box number.

The *Guide to Landed Estate Records* in PRONI contains an index to the Land Registry papers.

Newspaper reports of Land Courts

Another way for the family historian to access the records of the Irish Land Commission is through the pages of the local newspapers. The sittings of the Land Courts were reported in considerable detail. These include the cases of individual tenants who placed their cases before the Commissioners. The Commissioners' decisions are often followed by a list of tenants with the old rent and the new judicial rent given. Lists such as these can provide evidence that an ancestor lived on a particular estate towards the end of the nineteenth century.

Because so few newspapers are indexed, it is important to know something of the major Land Acts before approaching the microfilm collections to be found at one of the main libraries. These are set out below.

- 1870 Landlord and Tenant (Ireland) Act: This Act sought to compensate tenants for improvements made by them to their holding or for any disturbance to their occupancy. Tenants wishing to purchase the title to their property could borrow up to two-thirds of the price, which they could repay at 5% over 35 years.

- 1881 Land Law (Ireland) Act: This Act established the Land Commission and the Land Court.

- 1882 Amending Act: This Act empowered the Land Commission to cancel arrears of rent due by tenants of less than £30.

- 1885 Purchase of Land (Ireland) Act: Under the terms of this Act tenants were allowed to borrow the full amount of the purchase price, to be repaid over 49 years at 4%. Between 1885 and 1888 more than 25,000 tenants purchased their holdings.

- 1887 Land Act: This was an amendment to the 1881 Act extending the terms to leaseholders.

- 1896 Act: This amended the 1891 Land Act and empowered the Land Court to sell bankrupt estates to tenants.

- 1903 Land Act: This Act offered the landlords a 12% bonus if they agreed to sell out their entire estate. This Act, more than any other, brought about the transfer of the estates from the landlords to the tenantry.

Registry of Deeds

The Registry of Deeds was established by an Act of Parliament in 1708. The aim of the Act was to provide one central office in Dublin 'for the public registering of all deeds, conveyances and wills, that shall be made of any honours, manors, lands, tenements or hereditaments'. Researchers must remember that the act establishing the Registry of Deeds had its origin in the Penal Laws. From 1704 to 1780 no Catholic could purchase a lease for more than 31 years nor could a Catholic invest in mortgages. Also landowners were often apathetic about officially registering leases with their tenants, particularly those on smallholdings.

The deeds registered include leases, mortgages, marriage settlements and wills. This can provide the researcher with names, addresses and occupations of the parties involved as well as the names of those who acted as witnesses. During registration, which often took place years after the original transaction, a summary of the deed called a memorial was made. The details of the memorial were then copied into a large bound volume. It is these transcript volumes that are available for public inspection.

There are over 4 million memorials stored in the Registry of Deeds archive dealing with property in Ireland from its establishment. A memorial is a summary of a deed, and a description of the property and its location. Memorials are more often than not sufficiently detailed to substitute for original documents that may no longer be in existence.

A marriage settlement was the agreement made between the families of the bridge and groom prior to their wedding. The main aim was to provide financial security to the woman should she outlive her husband. The information in this type of deed varies, but can include the names and addresses of a large number of people from the two families involved. Occasionally the more detailed settlements include lists of names of tenants living on the lands of the groom's family.

In the era before banks were widespread, mortgages were commonly used as a ready means of raising capital, particularly by merchants and those seeking to buy land. They are not always easy to identify and their genealogical value can be fairly limited.

Rent charges were annual payments issuing from nominated lands and were used to pay off debts or provide for those family members without an adequate income.

A large number of wills were registered. A will was usually registered if there were concerns that it was going to be contested. Abstracts of over 2000 wills registered between 1708 and 1832 were published in three volumes by the Irish Manuscripts Commission (P.B. Phair and E. Ellis (eds), *Abstracts of Wills at the Registry of Deeds (1954–88)*).

Indexes to the deeds

Each deed registered was given its own individual reference number. In the indexes to the deeds the volume and the page are also given. For example, the reference 18.236.8764 means that this particular deed is on page 236 of volume 18 and is deed number 8764. This referencing system was used until 1832. After that the reference number includes the year in which the deed was registered.

Two indexes are available to the researcher: the *Index of Grantors* and the *Lands Index*. The format of the *Index of Grantors* has changed over the years. Before 1832 it gives the surname and the Christian name of the grantor, the surname of the grantee and the reference number. There is no indication of the location of the property concerned. After 1832 the *Index of Grantors* is more detailed and includes the county in which the property is located.

The *Lands Index* is arranged by county, with one or more counties per volume: the entries are arranged alphabetically, but only with regard to initial letter. Each entry gives the surnames of the parties, the name of the denomination of land, and the reference number. After 1828 the *Lands Index* is subdivided by barony. Additional references were often put at the end of books.

The Registry of Deeds is located in a large Georgian building in Henrietta Street, Dublin. The main entrance for vehicles is off Constitution Hill. The Registry is open Monday to Friday, 10.00 am to 4.30 pm and a small fee is charged for accessing the records. A member of staff will be on hand to offer help and advice. Although the layout of the building can be confusing, the arrangement of the records somewhat haphazard and the transcript volumes heavy and cumbersome, the Registry of Deeds is unlike any other archive in Ireland and is well worth a visit.

The *Index of Grantors* and the *Lands Index* are available on microfilm at the NLI, and PRONI has microfilms of both the indexes and the deeds (MIC/7 and MIC/311). A good guide to the Registry of Deeds is Jean Agnew's 'How to use the Registry of Deeds', in *Familia*, vol. 2, no. 6 (1990).

14 Church Records

The Church of Ireland

FROM 1537 UNTIL 1870 THE CHURCH OF IRELAND was the state Church (Established Church) in Ireland. Although it was initially committed to spreading Protestantism to the native Irish population, its congregations were made up mostly of English and Scottish settlers and officials. The vast majority of landowners were Anglican, and, outside Ulster, its membership consisted mostly of the professional classes. Fifty per cent or more of all barristers, solicitors, civil engineers, medical men, architects and bankers are listed in the 1861 census as members of the Church of Ireland.

There was a legal obligation for the Church of Ireland to keep records from 1634, although many rural parishes did not start to keep detailed records until the middle of the eighteenth century. Nevertheless, as a general rule the records of the Church of Ireland start much earlier than those of other Protestant denominations and of the Roman Catholic Church.

Registers

Parish registers of baptism, marriage and burial are the most important class of parish record available to researchers. They should not be neglected because an ancestor was of another denomination. Before 1782 it was not legal for Presbyterian ministers to perform marriages, and until 1844 they could not perform 'mixed marriages'. For this reason many marriages of other denominations, especially those classed as Dissenters, are recorded in the Church of Ireland registers.

The 1844 Act for Marriages in Ireland and for Registering such Marriages introduced the civil registration of Protestant marriages. These registers were kept in duplicate and a copy returned to the local registrar. From that date the information entered in the Church of Ireland marriage registers is the same as that contained in the records held at the General Register Office.

Burial registers are also of interest for families of other denominations because many Catholics and Dissenters were buried in Church of Ireland graveyards, if only for the very practical reason that in some areas the Established Church administered the only cemetery.

Under the Public Records Act 1867, an amendment of 1875 and the Parochial Records Act 1876, Church of Ireland parish registers of marriages prior to 1845 and of baptisms and burials prior to 1871 were declared to be public records. However, registers could be retained in parochial custody if an adequate place of storage was available. Almost half of the surviving registers held in Dublin were destroyed in 1922 and others have been lost at earlier periods. However, much of the lost information survives in transcripts and abstracts. The registers of 637 parishes in local custody survived, and in addition transcripts of or extracts from destroyed registers are available.

The NAI is in the process of completing the making of microfilm copies of surviving Church of Ireland parish registers, but not all of these are yet accessible to the public. PRONI holds microfilm copies of nearly all surviving registers for Northern Ireland. A growing number of surviving original registers is in the Representative Church Body Library in Dublin while others remain in local parochial custody.

The standard, but by no means complete, guide is the NAI *Guide to Parochial Records of the Church of Ireland* (typescript), a partly updated version of which is *A Table of Church of Ireland Parochial Records and Copies*, edited by Noel Reid (Naas 1994). See also *An Irish Genealogical Source: Guide to Church Records*, Belfast (1974). For further information see Raymond Refausse 'Records of the Church of Ireland', in *Irish Church Records*, edited by J.G. Ryan (Dublin, 1992). John Granham lists surviving records parish-by-parish at www.ireland.com/ancestor/browse/counties/index.htm.

Vestry minutes

In Ireland it was the Church of Ireland that administered the parish and these parishes became the units of local government. The concept of an Established Church meant that every person in the parish was considered to be a parishioner regardless of denomination, even if he or she did not worship at the local parish church.

The vestry meeting held annually on Easter Tuesday was therefore a meeting of all the inhabitants of the parish. The vestry could raise funds for local services such as poor relief, parish constables, road repair, the organization of education and the provision of recruits for the army.

Vestry minute books often contain items such as the names of the churchwardens, of the confirmed, of cess applotters and cess payers, of the poor, the widowed and the orphaned receiving relief, and of overseers of the poor and of the roads. They also include details of individuals who were not baptised, married or buried in the parish but who were of some significance locally. Vestry minute books are therefore a useful substitute for parishes which have no surviving registers.

Inevitably vestry records are richest for the cities and large towns; vestry records for rural parishes tend to be less rewarding. Some surviving vestry minute books have been deposited in the Representative Church Body Library and the PRONI.

Church Temporalities Commission

The Church Temporalities Commission was set up after the disestablishment of the Church of Ireland in 1869. Its function was to administer the revenues and property – including large estates with many tenants – of the Established Church. The Land Commission took over functions and records in 1881.

The Church Act of 1869 financed the state-aided purchase of Church lands by their tenants. About 6000 families took advantage of the legislation. Records for the Republic of Ireland are held by the NAI. They are not, however, available to the public at present as they have not been examined, listed and arranged by archivists.

PRONI holds the records of the Church Temporalities Commission for Northern Ireland, reference number FIN/10/10. Mortgages make up the great bulk of PRONI's holding of Church Temporalities documents. The remainder of the archive, about 50%, is made up of orders merging tithe rent charges, grants in perpetuity, schedules, copy deeds, indentures and conveyances (often between a purchaser, i.e., a tenant, and a member of the clergy).

Marriage licence bonds

The Prerogative and Consistorial or Diocesan Courts could issue marriage licences to those who did not wish to pursue the method of having banns called. The original marriage licences and accompanying bonds were destroyed in 1922, but the Prerogative and Diocesan indexes to the bonds have survived, and for convenience are shelved with the testamentary indexes at the NAI. The *Betham Abstracts* contain details of Prerogative marriage licences 1629–1801 and of Dublin Diocese marriage licences 1660–1824. Abstracts of Killaloe Diocese licences are held in the Genealogical Office, and abstracts of Ossory Diocese licences in the Representative Church Body Library. From 1845 the state registered non-Catholic marriages, and from 1864 marriages of all denominations were registered. PRONI also holds indices to the Marriage Licence Bonds.

The Roman Catholic Church

Roman Catholicism is the overwhelmingly predominant creed in Ireland. In 1887, Paschel Grousset, an exiled French journalist, noted that the Catholics he met were:

Catholics not so only in name. The greater number follow the services of the Church, observe all the rites, maintain a direct and constant intercourse with priests. The sincerity of their faith is particularly striking, and is not to be found in the same degree even in Italy or in Spain.

The Penal Laws were a series of enactments of the late seventeenth and early eighteenth centuries designed to remove the rights of Catholics to public office and to careers in certain professions. In spite of the Penal Laws, Catholic priests and bishops operated freely in most areas. Nevertheless, the Penal Laws militated against the erection of chapels and regular record-keeping. Roman Catholic registers therefore generally date from a later period than the equivalent Church of Ireland records, the majority dating from the 1820s.

Roman Catholic parishes are often made up of parts of more than one civil parish. Also, most Roman Catholic parishes have more than one church. Sometimes only one register was kept for the entire parish, but at other times each church had its own register. Starting dates for Roman Catholic parish records vary from one part of the country to the other. They start earliest in the cities with those for some city parishes in Dublin, Galway, Waterford, Cork and Limerick dating back to the late eighteenth century. Many of the registers in rural districts in the west of Ireland do not begin until the middle of the nineteenth century.

The main information given in baptism records is date, names of both parents (including the mother's maiden name, a custom not followed by Church of Ireland records), the names of two sponsors or godparents (often grandparents or other relatives) and sometimes (not always, alas) the place of abode (which is very useful when trying to locate individual families with a name common in the district). Illegitimate births are faithfully recorded.

The main information given in marriage records is date of marriage, place (the church in which the ceremony took place), names of both parties (including the bride's maiden name) and the names of two witnesses (often parents or other family, or best friends). The abode of the couple's parents is not always given. This latter situation improves in the 1860s with the introduction of new registers which have a column for address. Some priests had been careful to record addresses before this, but in general this is not the case. The same goes for baptism records.

Death or burial records were not well kept in Catholic parishes. The same register was generally used for births, marriages and deaths. Church of Ireland records of deaths and burials are much more thorough and extensive.

Where to find the registers

The registers remain the property of the Roman Catholic Church. Most of them are on microfilm (to 1880) at the NLI. Few of these are indexed. The NLI has produced a list of the parish registers which can be consulted on microfilm in the library. Parishes are listed alphabetically by diocese and the dates of the registers in each parish and the NLI call number are given. Please note that call numbers are not given for the Diocese of Cashel and Emly or for the Diocese of Kerry. This is because permission from the diocese is needed to view the films of these registers.

PRONI has microfilm copies for parishes in Ulster. They are to be found under MIC/1D. In addition there are some copies under CR/2.

The Franciscan Petition lists for Co. Armagh 1670–71

Although the hearth money rolls remain the main genealogical source for the seventeenth century, the Franciscan Petition lists should not be neglected for they contain the names of individuals in County Armagh that are not found in any other archive.

The records themselves relate to a dispute between the Franciscans and the Dominicans that had its origins in the 1640s. During the seventeenth century the Dominicans, as a result of their increasingly membership, had come into conflict with the Franciscans over their respective rights over the collection of alms or donations. The majority of the clergy and laity in Ulster supported the Franciscans and elected members of the congregation to represent their views to the Lord Primate, Oliver Plunkett.

The Franciscan Petition lists, therefore, contain the names of the clergy, gentry and parishioners of various townlands and parishes within the Armagh Diocese.

The complete list for the Diocese of Armagh has been published by Patrick J. Campbell, in *Seanchas Ardmhacha*, Journal of the Armagh Diocesan Historical Society, vol. 15, no. 1 (1992).

Convert rolls, 1703–1838

In order to convert the person read their renunciation of Catholicism in front of a clergyman and congregation at a public service. They then got a certificate from the bishop of the diocese saying they were a convert and enrolled it in the Court of Chancery. The bishop's certificate was necessary until 1782. From there on it was enough for the convert to receive the Sacrament from a minister of the Church of Ireland, take the oath before him and file a certificate to that effect in the Court of Chancery.

The convert rolls were destroyed in the fire in 1922. But they had been calendared and recorded (as were so many other documents). The calendar is in two volumes. Volume 1 covers the years 1703–1789 and has about 5500 names and Volume 2 covers 1789–1838 with 380 names and of these there were only 73 between 1800 and 1838.

Eileen O'Byrne's *The Convert Rolls* (Irish Manuscripts Commission, 1981) contains a list of those who converted during 1703–1838, the bulk of the entries dating from 1760 to 1790.

The Presbyterian Church

Presbyterianism came to Ireland from Scotland with the first plantation of Ulster during the early seventeenth century. In the first half of the seventeenth century the Church of Ireland contained several Scottish bishops who were prepared to ordain men of strong Calvinist theology, and several of them served in the parishes of the estates owned by Hamilton and Montgomery. In 1642, however, when a Scottish army came to Ulster to defend its people against the Irish rebels, it established the first formal presbytery in Ulster and claimed the right to take control over the whole area controlled by the army. Ministers were brought from Scotland, riding from parish to parish. Patrick Adair, one of these Scottish ministers, claimed that: 'The people were hungry in receiving the Gospel'.

Congregations of Presbyterian settlers were established during the Cromwellian period at Athlone, Clonmel, Dublin, Limerick and Mullingar. Despite the Presbyterian Church's support for the Williamite cause in Ireland during the 1690s, the government and bishops soon renewed their attack on it. Its freedom of action was severely curtailed by the Penal Laws, so that it was technically illegal for Presbyterian ministers to perform marriages of members of their congregation until 1782 and it was not until 1845 that they could legally marry a Presbyterian and a member of the Church of Ireland. These laws did not prevent Presbyterianism from becoming the predominant denomination in Down: by 1861 Presbyterians made up 44.5% of the population of the county.

Each Presbyterian congregation kept registers of baptisms and marriages: in general, they start later than those of the Church of Ireland. Additional Presbyterian records available for consultation at PRONI include session books, communicants' rolls and lists of members who emigrated. Because Presbyterians rarely kept burial registers, gravestone inscriptions provide valuable information that cannot be found elsewhere. It is also worth looking at Church of Ireland registers for baptisms, marriages and burials involving Presbyterians.

Another feature of Presbyterianism is the number of places that have more than one Presbyterian church, referred to as 1st, 2nd and 3rd. This, together with the fact that congregations tended to split or secede, makes life somewhat difficult for the researcher.

Presbyterian records copied by PRONI are available under MIC/1P and CR/3.

A good place to start your research for Presbyterian ancestors is the Presbyterian Historical Library located at Church House (Room 218), Fisherwick Place, Belfast. The library has many manuscripts relating to Presbyterian families and baptismal and marriage records of Presbyterian churches throughout Ireland.

The Non-Subscribing Presbyterian Church

The Non-Subscribing Presbyterian Church was formed in 1725 when a number of ministers and congregations refused to subscribe to the Westminster Confession of Faith, the statement of doctrine of the Presbyterian Church. Some of the early Non-Subscribing Presbyterian Church records, created before the split, are in fact Presbyterian records: for example, the early records of Scarva Street Presbyterian Church in Banbridge are to be found in Banbridge Non-Subscribing Presbyterian Church records. Non-Subscribing Presbyterian Church records can be found in PRONI under the reference code MIC/1B or CR/4.

The Reformed Presbyterian Church

The Covenanter or Reformed Presbyterian Church was composed of those who adhered most strongly to the Covenants of 1638 and 1643 and who rejected the Revolution Settlement of 1691 in Scotland. It was not until the latter part of the eighteenth century that congregations began to be organized and ministers were ordained. The earliest records begin mainly in the mid-nineteenth century, apart from some early nineteenth century sessions for Cullybackey, Co. Antrim, and Drumolg, Co. Londonderry. Some have been copied by PRONI and can be found under the reference codes MIC/1C and CR/5.

The Methodist Church

In 1738 John Wesley and his brother Charles started the movement that soon acquired the name of Methodism. John Wesley made his first visit to Ulster, where the movement had already established itself in many of the major towns, in 1756. He made regular visits to Ulster for the rest of his life. He spoke at local market houses or session houses and held open-air services. Occasionally sympathetic ministers would allow him to speak at the local meeting-house. However, not even the Earl of Moira could persuade the rector in the village to allow Wesley to speak at the parish church. Such was their interest in Wesley's teachings that, for a time, the Earl and Countess of Moira opened the great hall of their mansion for weekly public services conducted by Methodist preachers.

The majority of Methodists had been members of the Established Church and they remained members of their own local churches. Therefore they continued to go to the parish church for the administration of marriages, burials and baptisms. In 1816 a split developed between the Primitive Wesleyan Methodists, who retained their links with the Established Church, and the Wesleyan Methodists, who allowed their ministers to administer baptisms.

The majority of Methodist baptism and marriage registers do not begin until the 1830s and 1845 respectively. There are very few Methodist burial registers, because Methodist churches rarely had their own burial grounds. However, an important record is a large volume of baptismal entries for Methodist churches throughout Ireland deriving from the administrative records of the Methodist Church in Ireland (PRONI MIC/429/1), which may have been the product of an attempt to compile a central register of baptisms. Although incomplete, it contains baptisms from 1815 to 1840 that often pre-date the existing baptismal registers of Methodist churches.

The Religious Society of Friends

The Religious Society of Friends, also known as 'Quakers' or 'Friends', originated in the north-west of England in the mid-seventeenth century. The Quaker movement was brought to Ireland by William Edmundson when he established a business in Dublin in 1652. Initially the Quaker movement in Ireland was almost entirely confined to English settlers, many of whom had come to the country with the Cromwellian armies. The first concentrations were in Ulster, the richer agricultural areas in central Leinster, isolated small urban centres like Wicklow and Carlow and the major coastal trading cities such as Dublin, Cork, Waterford and Limerick.

Most of the early Quakers were engaged in agriculture and the linen trade. Later persecution for not paying tithes discouraged them from continuing as farmers. By the mid-eighteenth century most Irish Quakers were artisans, shop-keepers, merchants, and professional people.

The Quakers in Ireland are particularly associated with the work they did during the Great Famine. For as many stood idly by, the Quakers set up a sophisticated relief organization which became the forerunner for relief operations which continue in various parts of the world until this day.

From the beginning Quakers were among the best record-keepers Records include registers of births, marriages and deaths, minutes of meetings, accounts of sufferings and charity papers. As a result, Quaker records contain a great deal of information about local affairs.

The records are divided between the Society of Friends Historical Library, Dublin and the Quaker library at the Friends Meeting House, Railway Street, Lisburn, Co. Antrim. Records dating from the seventeenth century have been copied by PRONI and can be found under MIC/16.

The Moravian Church

The Moravians had their origin in a pre-Reformation Protestant Church called the Unitas Fratrum or United Brethren, a Hussite movement which arose in Moravia and Bohemia in what is now the Czech Republic. The Brethren underwent a revival in the 1720s and because so many of their members were from the region, they became known as the Moravians.

The Moravians arrived in England during the 1730s and some Dublin citizens on business in London in 1744 were so impressed with the preaching of John Cennick that they invited him to Dublin. He came to Dublin in 1746 and preached at first at the Baptist meeting-house in Skinner's Alley. He then moved northwards and in the succeeding years preached with considerable success in Antrim, Armagh, Derry and other counties. There were soon Moravian societies in most Ulster counties. From these sprang the congregations making up the Moravian Church in Ireland – Ballinderry, Kilwarlin, Cracehill, Cracefield, Belfast (University Road and Cliftonville) and Dublin. The Moravians had less impact outside the North and Dublin, but did establish some congregations in Counties Galway and Clare.

Apart from baptism, marriages and burial registers, the Moravian Church also maintains very detailed membership registers recording for each member date of birth, previous denomination, when deceased or left and the reason for leaving. Ministers' diaries contain births, marriages and deaths, the names of those who joined the church and those who left and lists of members.

PRONI has copied all the records held at Gracehill Moravian church which comprise not only those for Gracehill but also those for other churches including the Dublin church. All these records can be found under the reference code MIC 1F.

The Baptist Church

Baptists trace their origin from John Smyth (1554–1612), a Separatist exile in Amsterdam who, in 1609, reinstated the 'Baptism of conscious [adult] believers' and thereby reaffirmed his belief in the individual's responsibility for his or her soul. Although the Baptists were among the independent Churches that came into Ireland in the mid-seventeenth century, it was the nineteenth century before they began to make progress in Ulster. The earliest records in PRONI's custody begin in the 1860s and consist of marriages and minute books. As the Baptist Church does not practise infant baptism, there are no baptism registers indicating births, but details of those who came into membership can be found in the minute books. The Baptists do not have any burial grounds, hence the absence of burial registers.

Baptist Church records remain in local custody or with the Baptist Union of Ireland, 117 Lisburn Road, Belfast. Family historians should contact either the Public Record Office or check the local directory for the location and number of the relevant church.

Congregational Church

Although the Congregationalists came to Ireland as early as the seventeenth century few records exist before the 1880s. An exception to this rule are those of Richhill Congregational Church, whose baptismal records date from 1846 and lists of members from *c*.1848. These records are deposited in PRONI, reference CR/7/7.

Huguenot records

Savage religious persecution in their native country drove French Calvinists, known as Huguenots, abroad in large numbers. Some 10,000 made their way to Ireland, where they were welcomed by the Ascendancy for their Protestantism and for their industry. For three or four generations they sustained themselves as a distinct group but were gradually absorbed into the greater community. They made a significant contribution to Irish culture.

The most important Huguenot settlement in Ulster was founded in Lisburn (Lisnagarvey). William III's Bill to foster the linen trade in 1697 resulted in more than seventy French families, led by Louis Crommelin, migrating to establish the industry in Lisburn. Some refugees who arrived before 1704 attended the Church of Ireland in Lambeg or Lisburn Cathedral, both of whose registers contain many Huguenot names. The actual Huguenot registers were lost in the mid-nineteenth century and all subsequent efforts to trace them have failed. Many Huguenot names appear in the local Church of Ireland registers. For example, the burial entries for Christ Church Cathedral, Lisburn, show a large number of military funerals in 1689, when the Duke of Schomberg quartered his troops in Lisburn.

The Huguenot Society

The Huguenot Society of Great Britain and Ireland was established in 1885 to collect and publish information relating to the history and genealogy of Huguenots. The Huguenot Library at University College, Gower Street, London WC1, contains much material on Irish Huguenot families not available elsewhere, including manuscripts, pedigrees and collections of family papers.

An Irish section of the Society was established in 1987. All members of the Society receive a copy of *Huguenot Proceedings*, a useful work of reference for the family historian. An Annual General Meeting is held in Ireland each year and a church service, in St Patrick's Cathedral, Dublin, is held each November. Most Huguenots conformed, in due course, to the Church of Ireland. For this reason, the Irish section of the Huguenot Society has placed its archive in the Representative Church Body Library in Dublin.

Jewish records

Jews have lived in Ireland since at least the Middle Ages. In 1290 Jews were expelled from the dominions of the English Crown. They began to resettle in England from 1656 and in Ireland by the 1660s. Dublin had a rabbi by 1700 and a Jewish cemetery opened in 1718. By the middle of the eighteenth century Cork also had an organized community. Proposals to permit their naturalization were debated in the Irish parliament on four occasions between 1743 and 1747 but were rejected each time. The Irish Naturalization Act of 1784 explicitly excluded Jews, a provision repealed only in 1816.

By 1816 there were said to be only two Jewish families in Dublin. From the 1820s a new Jewish population appeared, mostly of German and Polish origin but coming to Ireland via England. A high proportion were goldsmiths, silversmiths, watchmakers or merchants. The numbers remained small, with only 393 Jews in 1861 and only 285 in 1871. From the 1880s numbers were reinforced from eastern Europe, mainly because of persecution in Tsarist Russia, and the present community is around 3000.

The Irish Jewish Museum

The Irish Jewish Museum is located in Portobello, around South Circular Road, Dublin 8. The former Walworth Road Synagogue there fell into disuse and ceased to function in the mid-1970s. The premises remained locked for almost ten years and were brought back to life again with the establishment of the Irish Jewish Museum Committee in late 1984. The museum contains a substantial collection of memorabilia relating to the Irish Jewish communities and their various associations and contributions to present-day Ireland. The material relates to the last 150 years and is associated with the communities of Belfast, Cork, Derry, Dublin, Limerick and Waterford.

15 Military Records

BEFORE THE UNION WITH GREAT BRITAIN IN 1801, Ireland had a separate army with its own organization and establishment (although the British Army drew heavily on Irish recruits). From 1801, Ireland remained a separate command, and the Irish regiments retained their Irish identity, but the Irish Army was merged with the British Army. Ireland was a popular recruiting area for the British Army over the centuries. Many young men with a taste for adventure or the desire to escape unemployment at home served in various regiments throughout the empire.

It was customary before the First World War for regiments to recruit primarily within a local district. The market town of Enniskillen, once one of the principal strongholds of the Ulster Plantation, has the unique distinction of giving its name to two of the oldest and most famous regiments of the British Army: the 27th Foot (known as the Royal Inniskilling Fusiliers) and the Royal Inniskilling Dragoons.

The Royal Irish Fusiliers recruited in the counties of Armagh, Louth, Cavan and Monaghan, the Royal Irish Rifles in the counties of Antrim, Down and Louth. The Munster Fusiliers were closely associated with the counties of Cork, Kerry, Limerick and Clare as their recruiting area, and Tralee as their depot. The Connaught Rangers recruited in the west of Ireland. On 3 October 1793 an advertisement was placed in the *Connaught Journal* under the caption 'God Save The King' and asking:

> *All spirited young men desirous of entering into the Royal Regiment of Connaught Rangers are desired to apply immediately to Captain Henry Shewbridge at Portumna; the Reverend Armstrong Kelly, Portumna Castle, or to Mr. Bricknell at Loughrea. Great encouragement will be given as non-commissioned officers to any properly qualified young men of the late*

Volunteer Corps, or who have lately quit his Majesty's services with good characters. Wanted – some drummers and fifers, etc.

Shortly afterwards the *Connaught Journal* was able to report:

A recruiting party of the Connaught Rangers, raised by the Hon. Colonel de Burgh, have beat up in Galway within these part few days, and we have no doubt from the encouragement given by the illustrious Commander under whom they are to act, but that this Corps will be complete in a very short time.

National Archives, London

Of course many Irishmen joined English regiments. The National Archives, London has records for men and women who left the services before the end of 1920. It is important that you know when your ancestor was in the forces and the regiment or unit with which they served.

For the nineteenth century the National Archives, London has several series of records detailing the service of officers and an alphabetical card index to these records is available. Correspondence about the sale and purchase of commissions between 1793 and 1871 is held in series WO 31. This contains a great deal of valuable genealogical information.

Records of military commissions and appointments of Irish officers between 1768 and 1877 are in HO 123. For information on ancestors who served in the rank and file the most useful records are the soldiers' documents in series WO 97.

Records relating to the Army in Ireland, 1775–1923, are in WO 35. Muster rolls of the Irish militia, 1793–1876, are in WO 13. The Royal Kilmainham Hospital, founded in 1679, acted as a hospital for disabled soldiers (known as in-pensioners) and also distributed money to out-pensioners: there are registers of in- and out-pensioners in the admission books, 1704–1922 (WO 118), and discharge documents, 1783–1822 (WO 119).

Other Irish soldiers and sailors had their pensions paid by the Royal Chelsea Hospital or by Greenwich Hospital. Records of these pensions, 1842–1862 and 1882–1883, are in WO 22/141-205 and WO 22/209-225. They can be used to trace changes of residence and dates of death. The only separate naval records for Irishmen are of nominations to serve in the Irish Coastguard, 1821–1849 (ADM 175/99-100).

For a more complete list see Simon Fowler's *Tracing Your Army Ancestors* (Pen & Sword Books, 2006) and *Army Service Records of the First World War* (Countryside Books, 2003).

General Register Offices, Dublin and Belfast

The General Register Office in Dublin has some records relating to Irish service personnel. These include records of deaths in the First World War, and returns of births, marriages and deaths of Irish persons at military stations abroad between 1881 and 1921. Similar material for Northern Ireland from 1930 is at the General Register Office in Belfast.

Commonwealth War Graves Commission Debt of Honour Register

Researchers interested in ancestors who died in the First or Second World War should consult the excellent website produced by the Commonwealth War Graves Commission. It contains more than 1.7 million names, at www.cwgc.org/cwgcinternet/search.aspx.

A photograph of 'Uncle Geordie Ryan' kept by my late grandmother had always puzzled me. He is photographed in military uniform with a rifle slung casually over his right shoulder. All that I could find out was that he had emigrated to Canada, joined a Canadian regiment and died during the First World War. Thanks to the War Graves Commission website I was able to find out that he had served in the Manitoba Regiment and died on 5 March 1918 aged thirty-five. The son of Mr and Mrs George Ryan from Co. Armagh, he married Margaret who lived at 60 Whittier Avenue, Transcona, Manitoba. He is buried at the Barlin Communal Cemetery at Pas de Calais, France (Grave/Memorial reference II. E. 10).

Not all entries are so detailed. Nevertheless, it makes such a difference to know so much more about a man who grins mischievously from an old photograph taken more than eighty years ago!

The Royal Irish Fusiliers Regimental Museum

The museum is situated in Sovereign's House, a fine Georgian building dating from 1809, and the first house built on Armagh's Mall. It celebrates the history of the Royal Irish Fusiliers, which is closely associated with the city of Armagh. The museum has interpretative displays covering the history of the Regiment and the Armagh, Cavan and Monaghan Militias from 1793 to 1968. There are fine displays of uniforms, trophies, badges and medals. The museum is the proud owner of the VCs won by Robert Morrow and Geoffrey Cather. The archive includes contemporary letters/diaries, battalion war diaries and discharge papers. Also of interest are photograph albums, war diaries and regimental histories.

Address: Sovereign's House, The Mall, Armagh,
Northern Ireland, BT61 9DL
E-mail: rylirfusiliers@aol.com
Web: www.rirfus-museum.freeserve.co.uk

The Royal Inniskilling Fusiliers Regimental Museum

Situated in the magnificent setting of Enniskillen Castle, once the medieval stronghold of the Maguires, the museum is housed in the Castle Keep and has displays which span the history of the Regiment from its formation in 1689 up to modern times.

Address: The Castle, Enniskillen, Co. Fermanagh,
Northern Ireland, BT74 7HL

The Royal Ulster Rifles Regimental Museum

The Royal Ulster Rifles (formerly the Royal Irish Rifles) have over 4000 artefacts on show in the museum including uniforms, trophies, badges and medals, including the VC won by James Byrne. Also of interest are photograph albums, war diaries and a library.

Address: Regimental Headquarters, The Royal Irish Rifles,
5 Waring Street, Belfast, BT1 2EW

Militia

The militia was a force originally intended for home defence and was
a far older institution than the regular army. Although service in the
regular army was voluntary for much of its history, men were obliged
to serve in the part-time militia if they were selected in a local ballot.
Catholics began to enter the lowest ranks only late in the eighteenth
century.

Local constables were empowered to draw up lists of all the able-
bodied men in their area. A ballot was then held to decide which
of these men were to be called upon to serve. Peers, clergymen,
articled clerks, apprentices, and those who had served previously were
among those who were exempt. Also any man selected by the ballot
to serve could be excused if he could provide a suitable substitute.
Volunteers frequently prevented the raising of men by compulsion.
The local gentry who provided the militia high command used their
considerable influence to keep their militia regiments well supplied by
volunteer recruits.

In 1793 the revolutionary government of France declared war on
Great Britain and the Irish militia regiments were reorganized to
meet the threat posed by both France and the United Irishmen.
These regiments were embodied more or less continuously until the
defeat of Napoleon in 1815. For the most part they were employed
on garrison duty in various parts of Ireland and provided drafts of
volunteers to the regular army. They also played an important role
during the 1798 Rebellion in Ireland.

All the militia regiments were re-embodied in 1855 when war broke
out in the Crimea. Once again they were generally used for garrison
duties, which freed the regular army for duty in the Crimea. In 1881 as
part of a general reorganization of the army all militia regiments were
reclassified as battalions of regular army regiments but retained their
militia status. The last period of embodiment for these battalions was

the Boer War (1899–1902). During the First World War they were used for recruitment and training.

Militia muster rolls for Ireland between 1793 and 1876 are held by the National Archives, London, reference WO 13. They are arranged by county and list alphabetically men's names, their ages and parish. Irish militia records are also held at the following locations:

Belfast

◆ List of Belfast Militia Company, May 1692, Trinity College Ms 1178
◆ Returns of Belfast Militia, May 1692, Ulster Museum Acc. 145-1950

Co. Antrim

◆ Payments to the Antrim Militia, Jan 1691; List of Officers of Antrim Militia, May 1692, Trinity College Ms 1178
◆ Lists of Antrim Militia Corps, 1760, Dublin Royal Irish Academy Ms 24k.19
◆ Militia Officers, 1761, PRONI T/808/15235
◆ Militia Pay Lists and Muster Rolls, 1799–1800, PRONI T.1115/1A & B

Co. Armagh

◆ Militia Officers, 1761, PRONI T.808/15235
◆ Militia Lists by Parish in the Barony of O'Neil Land West, 1793–5, PRONI D.1928/Y/1
◆ Militia Pay Lists and Muster Rolls, 1799–1800, PRONI T. 1115/2A-C
◆ List of Officers of Armagh Militia, 1808, PRONI T/561
◆ Muster Rolls, Armagh Militia, 1793–1797, PRONI D/183

Co. Cavan

◆ Militia List, 1761, GO 680

Co. Cork

◆ Militia List, 1761, GO 680

Co. Donegal

◆ Militia List, 1761, GO Ms 680

Co. Down

◆ Militia Officers, 1761, PRONI T/808/15235
◆ Oath and List of Names of Ballyculter Supplementary Corps, 1798, PRONI T/1023/153

Co. Dublin

◆ Militia List, 1761, GO 680

Co. Fermanagh

◆ Notebooks containing List of Fermanagh Militia, April 1708, NLI Ms 2696
◆ Militia Officers, 1761, PRONI T.808/15235
◆ Militia Pay Lists and Muster Rolls, 1794–99, PRONI T.1115/5A-C

Co. Kerry

◆ Militia List, 1761, GO 680

Co. Limerick

◆ Militia List, 1761, GO 680

Co. Londonderry

◆ Militia Officers, 1761, PRONI T/808/15235, GO 680

Co. Louth

◆ Militia List, 1761, GO 680

Co. Monaghan

◆ Militia List, 1761, GO 680

Co. Roscommon

◆ Militia List, 1761, GO 680

Co. Tipperary

◆ Militia List, 1761, GO 680

Co. Tyrone

◆ Militia Officers, 1761, PRONI T/808/15235
◆ Pay Roll of the Aghnahoe Infantry, 1829–32, PRONI D/1927

Co. Wicklow

◆ Militia List, 1761, GO 680

Yeomanry

The Yeomanry was formed in September 1796 under the threat of imminent invasion from France. The local gentry and magistrates throughout Ireland were empowered to raise infantry companies and cavalry troops in order to maintain a military presence in the absence of troops and militia called upon to intercept any invasion. The government paid, clothed and armed this volunteer force and their main function was to free the regular army and militia from their local peacekeeping activities. Service was usually two days per week and members were expected to turn out during emergencies.

Despite the intentions of the government the Yeomanry became a largely Protestant force in Ulster and after the Union of 1800 with Great Britain it remained a powerful symbol of Protestant determination to retain control of law and order in the North. The formation of the County Constabulary and a decade later the Irish Constabulary removed the need for such as peacekeeping force but the Yeomanry lingered on until it was officially disbanded in 1834.

The names of those local grandees who commanded local militia and yeomanry regiments were published during the eighteenth and nineteenth century. Lists are available at major libraries such as the Linen Hall Library and Central Library in Belfast or the local Irish History Libraries supported by the Education and Library Boards. On the shelves of the Linen Hall Library, for example, there are more than 200 volumes of army, navy and militia lists giving local and national information.

Muster books for the Yeomanry are held at the National Archives, London (WO 13/4059-4159). They are arranged by county and then by corps. They name the men and give their dates of service. Sadly they are available only from 1823 to 1834.

Various repositories in Ireland also hold yeomanry lists and related material. The most important are:

Co. Antrim
◆ List of Yeomanry Corps, 1804, RAI Ms 24k.19

Co. Armagh
◆ Crowhill Yeomanry Pay List, c.1820, PRONI T/2701
◆ Ardress Yeomanry Book, c.1796, PRONI D/296
◆ Churchill Yeomanry Book, c.1796, PRONI D/321/1

Co. Down
◆ Killyleagh Yeomanry List, 1798, PRONI D/303
◆ Mourne Yeomanry Lists, 1824, PRONI T/991

Co. Fermanagh
◆ Yeomanry Muster Rolls, 1797–1804, PRONI T/808/15244

Co. Londonderry
◆ Yeomanry Muster Rolls, 1797–1804, PRONI T/1021/3

General

◆ Extracts of Regular Army Muster Rolls, 1741–80, PRONI T/ 808/15196

Volunteers

The Volunteers were a part-time military force raised locally during 1778–1800, in companies and battalions. Members were drawn mainly from the Protestant middle classes and officers from the local gentry and aristocracy. Shortly after their formation the Volunteers adopted a more overtly political role as radical politicians took leading positions in the force.

By 1782 there were 40,000 enlisted in the Volunteers, half of them in Ulster. That same year the Volunteers played a major role in forcing the British government to concede the independence of the Irish Parliament. They then campaigned for the reform of the legislature itself and began to falter in 1784 as a result of the divisions caused by the question of Catholic emancipation.

Although the Volunteers lost their national importance, they continued to exist at a local level. Enthusiasm for joining did recover briefly after 1789 with the excitement caused by the French Revolution, but legislation prohibiting the import of arms and declaring illegal all assemblies for the purpose of soliciting a change in the law that claimed the status of a representative body effectively ended volunteering.

Muster rolls for volunteer regiments, including Irish regiments, are held by the National Archives, London, reference WO 13. They are arranged by county and list alphabetically men's names, their ages and parish.

16 Printed Sources

Ordnance Survey Memoirs

ORDNANCE SURVEY MEMOIRS PROVIDE a great deal of background information on the character and habits of the people who lived in Ireland during the early part of the nineteenth century. In 1824 a House of Commons committee recommended a townland survey of Ireland with maps at the scale of 6 inches to one statute mile to facilitate a uniform valuation for local taxation. The survey was directed by Colonel Thomas Colby, who had available to him officers of the Royal Engineers and three companies of sappers and miners. In addition, civil servants were recruited to help with sketching, drawing and engraving maps and eventually, in the 1830s, with the writing of the memoirs.

The memoirs are written descriptions intended to accompany the maps, containing information that could not be fitted on to them. They are a unique source for the history of the northern half of Ireland before the Great Famine, as they document the landscape and situation, buildings and antiquities, land-holdings and population, employment and livelihoods of the parishes. The surveyors recorded the habits of the people, their food, drink, dress and customs. Details of ruined churches, prehistoric monuments and standing-stones were also included.

The Ordnance Survey Memoirs contain much valuable information on ancient forts, settlements and graveyards. Of particular interest to the local historian is the information on local schools, churches and landed estates as well as descriptions of the towns and villages. Useful genealogical information can also be found. The memoirs for the

Parish of Hillsborough, Co. Down, for example, contain an extensive list of subscribers to the Hillsborough Charitable Society, which sought to provide food, clothing and shelter for the destitute poor.

Fascinating insights into the everyday life of our ancestors are provided, with descriptions of local dress or customs. Some information on local names can occasionally be found.

Where to find the records

Only the northern part of Ireland was covered before the scheme was dropped. In recent years the Institute of Irish Studies at The Queen's University of Belfast has published the Ordnance Survey Memoirs in 40 volumes as follows:

◆ Co. Antrim: vols 2, 8, 10, 13, 16, 19, 21, 23, 24, 26, 29, 32, 35 and 37
◆ Co. Armagh: vol. 1
◆ Co. Donegal: vols 38 and 39
◆ Co. Down: vols 3, 7, 12 and 17
◆ Co. Fermanagh: vols 4 and 14
◆ Co. Londonderry: vols 6, 9, 11, 15, 18, 22, 25, 27, 28, 30, 31, 33, 34 and 36
◆ Co. Tyrone: vols 5 and 20
◆ Counties Cavan, Leitrim, Louth, Monaghan and Sligo: vol. 40

The Ordnance Survey created huge quantities of archives, some of which have already been transferred to the NAI. These consist of part of the administrative archives, most of the archives generated by the mapping of the country at the scale of 6 inches to the mile (1: 10,560) and town plans at various scales.

The Ordnance Survey continues to hold a very large quantity of records which will be transferred to the NAI over the next few years. These consist of administrative records and records created in the survey or making of other maps at various scales, including 1 inch and 25 inch maps, as follows:

◆ OS Parish List: Index of over 2500 parish names
◆ OS 1: Progress reports and returns

- OS 2: Correspondence registers and indexes
- OS 3: Registered correspondence 1824–46 (not listed separately, see OS 2)
- OS 5: Registered correspondence 1847–90 (not listed separately, see OS 2)
- OS 6: Registered correspondence 1891–1935 (not listed separately, see OS 2)
- OS 7: Registered correspondence 1936–52 (not listed separately, see OS 2)
- OS 12: Engraving journals
- OS 13: Orders, circulars and memoranda
- OS 43: Parish observation books
- OS 51: Registers of documents
- OS 54: descriptions of trigonometrical stations
- OS 55: Boundary remark books
- OS 58: Content field books
- OS 59: Road field books
- OS 60: Levelling field books
- OS 62: Content registers originals
- OS 63: Content registers duplicates
- OS 65: Levelling registers originals
- OS 66: Levelling registers duplicates
- OS 95: Templemore memoir
- OS 96: Memoirs, places other than Templemore
- OS 102: Plots of rivers and lakes
- OS 103: Common plots
- OS 104: Plots
- OS 105: Fair plans
- OS 107: Proof impressions
- OS 140: Manuscript town plans
- Town Plans: Index of town plans (OS 138 to OS 146)

The Irish Academy, Dublin, holds the Ordnance Survey Letters, a collection of 40 volumes of manuscript letters, mainly written by John O'Donovan, MRIA (1801–1861), as he carried out fieldwork during the Ordnance Survey 6-inch mapping project during the period 1833 to 1846. Also of interest are the Ordnance Survey Memoir drawings, a collection of c.1000 drawings incorporated in the memoirs collected by soldiers working the Ordnance Survey 6-inch map project. Although the memoirs were published by the Institute of Irish Studies, The Queen's University of Belfast during the 1990s, most of the drawings were not included in the published version.

PRONI has in its custody microfilm copies of the Ordnance Survey Memoirs (MIC/6).

Street directories and almanacs

Street directories contain a great deal of information on the gentry, the professional classes, merchants, etc. They include information on even the smallest of market towns and ports in Ireland. Following a description of the town and surrounding countryside, the names and addresses of the local butchers, pawnbrokers, blacksmiths and coachbuilders are given, as well as the various places of worship, with the names of the local ministers, etc., and the location of local schools. Street directories can therefore be useful if you wish to find out which church or school your ancestor attended. The names and addresses of the local members of parliament, magistrates, poor law guardians and town commissioners are also included in many street directories. In fact the only classes that are excluded from directories are the small tenant farmers, landless labourers and servants.

Undoubtedly, the most complete collection of directories and almanacs is in the NLI. It also has microfilmed copies of the rare works.

Countrywide directories

◆ Ambrose Leet's *A Director to the Market Towns, Villages, Gentlemen's Seats, and other Noted Places in Ireland*, 1814, was one of the first general directories for all of Ireland. The principal countrywide directories which are invaluable to family historians are those published by James Pigot, Alexander Thom and J. Slater.

◆ Pigot's *Commercial Directory of Ireland, Scotland, etc.*, was published in 1820; a subsequent edition was published in 1824.

◆ *Thom's Irish Almanac and Official Directory*, published annually from 1844, until 1915, lists all members of parliament, the Irish Peerage, Baronets, Officers of the Army, Navy, Militia; members of government departments, all county officers; members of professional organizations and the professions of law, medicine, surgery, bankers, etc. The clergy of all denominations are also listed. Officers of universities, colleges, schools, etc., are also named. In fact, the lists cover all but the gentry who filled no public or professional position, the tradesmen, small farmers, and the lower classes.

◆ Slater's *National Commercial Directory of Ireland*, 1846, 1856, 1870, 1881 and 1894, is arranged under the four provinces. Each city, post and market town is represented with a list of its nobility, gentry and clergy. Members of all professions and trades are listed separately except under the smallest towns, for which they are grouped alphabetically with their occupations designated. In addition, for Dublin, Belfast, and Limerick, there is an alphabetical directory of the city and its suburbs, containing the names, occupation and address of every man listed in the classified section. Also included at the back of the volume are classified directories of the principal merchants, manufacturers, and traders of seven English cities and of Glasgow and Paisley, Scotland.

Dublin directories

◆ Wilson's *Dublin Directory*, which consists purely of alphabetical lists of merchants and traders, is the earliest for this city. It began in 1751 and was issued annually, except for the years 1754–9, until 1837.

◆ The *Gentleman's and Citizen's Almanack*, published by John Watson and later compiled by John Watson Stewart, began publication in Dublin in 1736, and continued to 1844. Known later as *The Treble Almanack*, it also consists of merchants and traders including bankers, dentists and physicians.

◆ Pettigrew and Oulton's *Dublin Almanac and General Register of Ireland*, which began annual publication in 1834, includes a street-by-street listing which was enlarged year by year to include Dublin's expanding suburbs. From 1835 an alphabetical list of the individuals recorded is also included.

Provincial directories

During the nineteenth century, a great many local directories were produced, particularly for important commercial centres such as Dublin, Cork, Limerick, Belfast, Londonderry and Newry, although the quality of these vary considerably from locality to locality. Of particular interest to anyone tracing his or her family tree are the following:

◆ John Ferrar's *Limerick Directory* was published in 1769. A copy is in the Limerick Public Library.

◆ Richard Lucas published *Lucas' Directory of Cork, and South-East Towns, Younghal to Kinsale*, 1787; 1821. He also published the *General Directory of Ireland*, 1788. This covers 27 towns of the south half of Ireland, not included in his 1787 *Directory*. These two directories of Lucas, being rare, have been microfilmed by the NLI.

◆ James Haly published a *Directory of Cork*, 1795.

◆ John Connor followed with a *Directory of Cork, c.*1829–30.

A wide range of directories are available for Belfast. These include the following:

◆ *Martin's Belfast Directory*, 1839 and 1841–2, includes an alphabetical list of gentry, merchants and traders living in Belfast and also a street-by-street listing of the principal streets.

◆ Matier's *Belfast Directory*, 1835–6 and *c.*1860, includes an alphabetical list of gentry, merchants and traders residing in Belfast and its neighbourhood.

◆ The *Belfast and Province of Ulster Directory*, published in various years from 1854 to 1947, includes a street-by-street listing for Belfast. The principal towns are represented with alphabetical lists of gentry, merchants and traders and the principal villages of Ulster consist of alphabetical lists of 'residents in vicinity'.

Many smaller guides are available for towns in Ireland. Some of the more valuable directories include:

- 1830 McCabe's *Drogheda Directory*

- 1839 T. Shearman's *New Commercial Directory for the Cities of Waterford and Kilkenny* . . .

- 1839 *Directory of the Towns of Sligo, Enniskillen, Ballyshannon, Donegal etc.*

- 1865 *Sligo Independent Almanac*

- 1872 George Griffith's *County Wexford Almanac*

- 1884 George Henry Bassett's *Kilkenny City and County Guide and Directory*

- 1885 George Henry Bassett's *Wexford County Guide and Directory*

- 1886 George Henry Bassett's *Louth County Guide and Directory*

- 1886 George Henry Bassett's *County Down Guide and Directory*

- 1888 George Henry Bassett's *County Armagh Guide and Directory*

- 1888 George Henry Bassett's *Antrim Guide and Directory*

- 1889 George Henry Bassett's *County Tipperary Guide and Directory*

- 1889 Francis Guy's *Postal Directory of Munster* (issued annually from 1889)

- 1889 *Sligo Independent Directory*

For more information on the large number of directories available see James Carty's *National Library of Ireland Bibliography of Irish History, 1870–1911* (Dublin, 1940) and Edward Evans' *Historical and Bibliographical Account of Almanacks, Directories etc. in Ireland from the Sixteenth Century* (Dublin, 1897), which include details of provincial directories.

Newspapers

Newspapers have been published in Ireland since the mid-seventeenth century. The oldest newspaper in the NLI's collection is *An Account of Chief Occurrences in Ireland*, published in February 1660 by Sir Charles Coote. It ran for only a few issues. The *Newsletter*, which was published in Dublin in 1685 and appeared twice a week for seven months, is closer to the modern concept of newspaper publication.

Although the first newspapers were published in the seventeenth century, it was not until the eighteenth century that the larger towns began to publish their own newspapers. Cork, Limerick and Waterford all published newspapers in the first few decades of the eighteenth century. The *Belfast Newsletter*, first published in 1737, is one of the oldest continuously published newspapers in the world.

These early newspapers can prove disappointing for family historians because they concentrated mainly on national and international news. Local news began to feature only later in the eighteenth century. They are useful, nevertheless, because they feature advertisements, obituaries, market prices and properties to let. By the early nineteenth century newspapers had become the most important medium of public opinion and information. At the same time, local newspapers increasingly covered local issues. Births, deaths and marriages were covered more frequently and, like obituaries, usually related to the higher echelons of society.

The minutes of the boards of guardians or town commissioners appeared after each meeting and, as a result, became regular features; they often contain the names of those who were elected or selected for local office. The proceedings of the assizes at the local courthouse were often reported in considerable detail. According to the *Irish Times* for 1 January 1900 the following cases were heard at the Northern Division Police Courts, Dublin:

WIFE-BEATING – James Brederick, an engine fitter, residing at 19 Cole's Lane, was charged with assaulting his wife. The accused had struck the women several times with his fist, knocked her down, and blackened one of her eyes. He was sentenced to three months' imprisonment with hard labour. Patrick Brien, a labourer, was sentenced to six months' imprisonment with hard labour for assaulting his wife, Mary Anne Brien by kicking her about the head and body so severely that she had to be treated in the Richmond Hospital.

Identifying newspapers

The drawback in using newspapers for genealogy is that you generally need to have a fairly precise date for an event before venturing to hunt for coverage, since indexes are limited. If you have the date of a marriage or a trial or a fatal accident you first need to find what newspapers were being published at the time in the relevant area. For this the essential source is *Newsplan Project in Ireland* (England, 1992), compiled by James O'Toole. This lists all newspapers published in Ireland with their dates of operation. It also has chronological lists of newspapers arranged by town of publication and by county, so it is easy to identify which papers were in existence in an area at a given time. Remember, however, to check under the names of adjoining counties, as local newspapers never respected invisible county boundaries. The Newsplan database is available online at www.nli.ie/newsplan/default.htm.

Local newspapers can be consulted in public libraries. They are often available only on microfilm and have rarely been indexed. Belfast Central Library holds a series of fully indexed cuttings books of articles derived from major local newspapers since 1898. The microfilm of this series spans the years 1898–1976. From 1976 the newspaper cuttings books are held in hard copy in the Irish and Local Studies Department.

Locations

The best single repository for Irish newspapers is the British Library. From 1826 it was obliged to hold a copy of all Irish publications from that date and its collection is virtually complete.

Within Ireland, the largest collection is held by the NLI. Under legal deposit law, a copy of each newspaper published in the Republic must be donated to the NLI. Northern Ireland newspapers are not covered by this legislation, but are received through donations or purchase. The collection covers titles published from the mid-seventeenth century to the present day. Irish titles are, of course, the primary focus of the collection. The policy is to collect all national, provincial and local newspapers with substantial news content published in Ireland and Northern Ireland, including free newspapers. Selected titles from other countries, including Irish newspapers published abroad, are also collected. The NLI receives around 300 titles annually. An online catalogue is available in their website.

Many unique copies are held in local libraries and other repositories.

Indexes

A number of indexes exist to the biographical material found in newspapers, which can greatly lighten the burden of research. Those dealing with single publications are as follows:

◆ NLI index to the *Fireman's Journal*, 1763–1771

◆ NLI index to marriages and deaths in *Pue's Occurrences* and the *Dublin Gazette*, 1730–40, NL MS. 3197

◆ Index to Henry Farrar's biographical notices in *Walker's Hibernian Magazine*, 1772–1812 (1889)

  ◆ Card indexes to the biographical notices in the *Hibernian Chronicle*, 1771–1802, and the *Cork Mercantile Chronicle*, 1803–1818, held by the Irish Genealogical Research Society in London

◆ Index to biographical material in the *Belfast Newsletter*, 1737–1800, held by the Linen Hall Library in Belfast

An index to birth, marriage and death entries in the *Belfast Newsletter, 1738–1864* is available at the Linen Hall Library. Before 1800 the index is bound in volumes in the genealogical reference area. From 1800 to 1864 it is a card index which has to be ordered up.

17 Law and Order

Policing

DESPITE A SERIES OF ACTS OF PARLIAMENT passed during the eighteenth century, the Irish police force at the time of the Act of Union of 1800 was still composed only of small groups of sub-constables. These part-time policemen, appointed by the grand juries, were few in number and poorly paid out of the county funds.

In 1787, an attempt had been made to provide a police force in Ireland. Known as 'Barnies', they quickly proved inadequate for the suppression of disturbances. Sir Robert Peel made another attempt in 1814 with the creation of the Peace Preservation Force. Known as 'Peelers', they could be called upon by the Lord Lieutenant for use in a district that had been 'proclaimed' as a disturbed area. This force proved inadequate too and in 1822 the County Constabulary was established. From 1822 there were two police forces in Ireland: the Peace Preservation Force worked in proclaimed districts and the County Constabulary work to maintain law and order throughout the rest of the country.

The passage of the Constabulary (Ireland) Act 1836 finally brought a single, unified force into being. Power to appoint and discharge members of the force, to make rules and to fix salaries was vested in the Lord Lieutenant of Ireland. The Irish Constabulary was responsible for the preservation of law and order throughout the country with the exception of Dublin. The Irish capital retained its own police, the Dublin Metropolitan Police, which had been formed in 1786. Members of the Constabulary, who were mainly Catholic, were recruited from among the tenant farmer class and were removed to distant stations. The force was unpopular in many areas because it was used to assist at evictions and because it supplied Dublin Castle with most of its intelligence information.

In September 1867, in recognition of its loyalty during the Fenian Rising, the Constabulary was renamed the Royal Irish Constabulary. The duties of the Constabulary were gradually extended. At first it was concerned solely with keeping the peace, a duty which could entail the suppression of armed rebellion, sectarian riots or agrarian disturbances; later it inherited the functions of the Revenue Police, made inquiries on behalf of departments of state, collected agricultural statistics, enforced the fishery laws and performed a variety of duties under the laws relating to food and drugs, weights and measures, explosives and petroleum. Members of the force also acted as enumerators at the censuses of population.

The Royal Irish Constabulary was disbanded on 30 August 1922. Pensions continued to be paid by the Paymaster General in London, and the service records of members of the force passed to the Home Office.

Records of service

The prime source is the Royal Irish Constabulary records in the National Archives, London (HO 184) The records are entered in registers arranged numerically by service number; there are separate, alphabetical indexes from which the service number can be obtained. Separate registers, with integral indexes, were compiled for officers and for members of the auxiliary forces. The registers normally give:

◆ full name;

◆ age;

◆ height;

◆ religious affiliation;

◆ native county;

◆ trade or calling;

◆ marital status;

◆ native county of wife;

◆ date of appointment;

◆ counties in which the man served;

◆ length of service;

◆ date of retirement and/or death.

The name of a wife is not given, nor any information about parents. The reference numbers quoted in these records refer to papers that have not survived.

Pensions and allowances granted to officers, men and staff, and to their widows and children, are recorded in the class Royal Irish Constabulary Pensions etc. (PMG 48). Entries in these registers are arranged either alphabetically in order of surname or by pension award number, and normally include the place of residence of the recipient. Pensions paid to dependants, commissioned officers and office staff are sometimes entered separately from those for members of the force.

This class also contains registers of deceased pensioners for the period 1877–1918, and rolls of pensions awarded on the disbandment of the force. Files on pension options at disbandment are arranged county by county: Dublin Castle records (CO 904), pieces 175 and 176. In some cases these provide addresses and information about service. Lists of officers recommended for pensions when the Constabulary was disbanded, arranged by districts with separate series for British and Irish recruits, are in HO 184, pieces 129–209; in most cases the information in these lists was entered into the general registers of service in this class.

A list of superannuations awarded to police in Ireland before the unified force was created was published in 1832 in House of Commons Sessional Papers 1831–1832, XXVI 465. The list gives:

◆ name;

◆ period of service;

◆ amount granted;

◆ nature of injury leading to the superannuation.

The Garda Museum and Archive

The police force in the Republic of Ireland is called the Garda
Siochana (in English the term means the 'guardians of the peace').
The force was set up in 1922 immediately after the establishment of
the Irish Free State. Garda headquarters is situated in the Phoenix
Park, Dublin, and it is home to the Garda Museum and Archives.

The most important item from the point of view of the family
historian is the *Numerical Register of the Officers and Men of All Ranks
in the Dublin Metropolitan Police*. This single volume has over 12,500
entries, each one giving important genealogical information about a
member of the force including:

◆ name;

◆ age;

◆ trade or occupation;

◆ parish;

◆ post town;

◆ divisions attached to while in the force and dates of joining each;

◆ removal from the force, cause and date.

The register begins in the year 1837 and continues up to March 1925.
A handwritten index is available with the surnames in alphabetical
order. It is important to note that the register has been microfilmed
and is available at the NAI.

Also of interest is *RIC Allocations Record 1902–21*, which gives details
of the locations to which RIC men were sent during that period. The
final section of this book seems to refer to members of the 'Black-
and-Tans'.

Irish Revenue Police

The records of the Irish Revenue Police are held by the National Archives, London. For Irish Revenue Police, 1830–57, who tried to prevent illicit distilling, try CUST 111. For Irish Excise Men, 1824–33, see CUST 110. For Customs officers in Ireland, 1682–1826, see CUST 20. There are pensions records in for 1785–1851 CUST 39/161. After this, try *Ham's Customs Year Book* and *Ham's Inland Revenue Year Book* in the PRO Library (1875–1930). These list Customs and Inland Revenue officials (up to 1923 for Ireland), and include a name index.

Researching in Northern Ireland

PRONI has microfilmed 44 volumes of registers of service of members of the RIC, 1816–1922 (ref. MIC 454). The entries are arranged numerically by service number and give:

◆ full name;

◆ age;

◆ height;

◆ religious affiliation;

◆ native county;

◆ trade or calling;

◆ marital status;

◆ native county of wife;

◆ date of appointment;

◆ counties in which the man served;

◆ length of service, etc.

Also of interest is a register of householders kept by the RIC for the subdistricts of Knocknacarry and Cushendall, 1801–1901 (T/3507). This volume contains a great deal of genealogical material including the names of individuals who are listed as 'gone to America' in June 1881.

The courts

For local crime the records of the petty sessions courts, which in most cases survive from the mid-nineteenth century, are useful. Where they are available, the manor court records will give details of cases of debt up to the value of 40 shillings. More serious crime was dealt with at the assize courts, and though many of the nineteenth-century records were destroyed in 1922 some isolated material has survived.

Crown and Peace records

Before the partition of Ireland, a Clerk of the Crown and Peace in each county maintained the records of the county court (court of quarter sessions) as well as the records of the assizes. The Clerk was also responsible for keeping the records of the grand jury, which are discussed in Chapter 18. Unfortunately the vast majority of these records for the South of Ireland were destroyed in Dublin in 1922. Most surviving court records in the NAI are from the twentieth century.

PRONI has Crown and Peace records dating mostly from the last quarter of the nineteenth century. Among the many classes are affidavits, appeals, civil bill books, convictions, crown files at assizes, voters' lists and registers. All of these contain information on people who were involved in the administration of the legal system, such as local police officers, solicitors and officers of the court, as well as those who had fallen foul of the law. The Crown books contain the names of the grand jury, a calendar of prisoners, the names of the defendants, witnesses and court officials.

The Crown books deal with crimes ranging from larceny to assault. Seasonal crimes are also well represented: Anne Reilly (also called Anne Fitzpatrick), for example, appeared before the Newtownbutler Court in December 1877 charged that she 'did steal take and carry away one domestic fowl to wit a goose of the value of 2/- of the goods of one Robert Maginess against peace'. She was sentenced to one calendar month's imprisonment without hard labour.

Also with the Crown and Peace archive are spirit licence registers. These contain the name and address of the trader and of the owner of the premises. Criminal injury books, which give details of individual claims for damages, include the name and address of applicant, solicitors, police officers and witnesses. The claims relate to such matters as the destruction of a building or crops by fire or the breaking of a plate-glass window in a local shop. The applicant claimed damages from the local county council and if these were awarded they were levied off the relevant townland or electoral division.

One of the most unusual collections to be found within the Crown and Peace archive contains the registers of trees. By the end of the seventeenth century a great deal of Ireland's natural woodland had been cut down and timber was beginning to be in short supply. The provisions of a 1765 Act, which stated that on the expiration of his lease, a tenant could claim for the trees he planted, or their value, provided he had lodged a certificate of the trees planted with the Clerk of the Crown and Peace for the county, resulted in registers of trees which have survived for various counties in Northern Ireland.

The registrations were recorded at the quarter sessions and published in the *Dublin Gazette*. Subsequently this information was entered in a ledger entitled *Register of Trees* in which, depending on the diligence of the Justice of the Peace, the original affidavits were copied out in full or summarized. This information can be of interest to genealogists researching a particular family who had long-established roots in a particular townland or county.

The Crown and Peace records for Co. Down date back to 1769, for Londonderry to 1773, for Antrim to 1841 and Tyrone to 1831. A separate catalogue exists in the Public Search Room for each of the six counties of Northern Ireland.

18 Local Government

Corporations

A CITY OR TOWN CORPORATION WAS A LOCAL administrative body formed for purposes of government by municipal officers. From medieval times, city or town corporations were created by Patent held of the Crown. Largely created by the Stuarts, the corporations in Ireland often performed no function apart from electing members of parliament. This was partly due the fact that many of them were responsible for little more than villages and partly because some, like Belfast Corporation, were dominated by powerful patrons.

A Municipal Reform Act of 1840 abolished the existing corporations, preserving borough councils in just ten places (Dublin, Cork, Limerick, Belfast, Londonderry, Drogheda, Kilkenny, Sligo, Waterford and Clonmel) – Wexford was incorporated later, in 1845. These corporate bodies comprised a mayor, aldermen and councillors: to be eligible for office, candidates were required to be on the burgess roll and possessed of property, real or personal, to the value of £1000 over and above any debts, or to be the occupier of a house rated for poor law purposes at £25 per annum.

Corporation records are held by local authority archives in the Republic or Ireland. The best guide to these is the *Directory of Irish Archives*, by Seamus Helferty and Raymond Refaussé. In Northern Ireland, corporation records are held by PRONI, reference LA. The earliest surviving records of Belfast Corporation were reprinted in *The Town Book of the Corporation of Belfast, 1613–1816*, edited by R.M. Young (Marcus Ward, 1892).

Town commissioners

The Lighting of Towns (Ireland) Act of 1828 established town commissions with responsibility for lighting and cleaning. More were established under the Towns Improvement Act (1854), which also gave them additional powers in the areas of cleaning and paving of streets; the prevention of fire; the safeguarding of the community from dangerous buildings; the regulation of traffic and the licensing of hackney carriages. Later Acts authorised town commissioners to establish and regulate markets, and gave them power to formulate housing schemes.

The town Commissioners' minute books provide a considerable amount of material that will be of interest to genealogists. Lists of names appear for a variety of reasons. Records for town commissioners in Northern Ireland are held in the local authority archive at PRONI. Those which survive for the Republic of Ireland are held largely held by local authority archives. A significant collection of material from Kilkee town commissioners, for example, is held by Clare County Archives, and Louth County Archives holds Ardee town commissioners' records. The best guide to these is the *Directory of Irish Archives*, by Seamus Helferty and Raymond Refausse.

Grand juries

In 1210, during the reign of King John, it was decided to divide Ireland into local administrative units, which were originally called shires, and later counties. Knights were given estates on the conquered lands and, in return, were to give services to the king in times of war and to pay certain dues. A king's officer was appointed in each shire or county to collect these contributions, visiting each county twice a year. He also summoned the feudal tenants to meet the king's visiting judges at the county town. From this gathering, he selected twenty-three of the chief landowners known as the grand jury.

By the eighteenth century, the grand jury was appointed yearly by the county High Sheriff and had both judicial and administrative responsibilities. Its judicial function was to preside at the assizes and examine bills of indictment relating to criminal matters. Administrative tasks were undertaken at presentment sessions. These special sessions were most often used for raising money for specific purposes such as the upkeep and building of roads and bridges and the supervision of workhouses, gaols, fever hospitals and other county institutions. Expenditure was financed through a system of local taxation known as the county cess.

Grand jury presentments are the chief records of the county administration prior to 1898. These and grand warrants contain information about work ordered to be done by the grand jury on roads, bridges and gaols and about constabulary duties in the counties. They are often arranged barony by barony within the county and useful genealogical information can be obtained by detailed searching of them. They are not indexed. Although frequently printed, different sets contain manuscript amendments and notes according to who owned and used them.

Also of interest are the lists of grand jurors, which include the names of qualified jurors, their places of residence and occupations (referred to in the lists as: title, quality, calling or business). The qualification for jury service from 1692 onwards was that jurors had to own property valued at £10 annually. In later Acts, substantial leaseholders were also included as jurors.

Grand jury records for Northern Ireland are held at PRONI. In the Republic of Ireland, they are divided between the NAI and local county archives. The following is a basic guide to surviving records and their locations:

Antrim	1711–1840; 1867–1895	PRONI
Armagh	1758–1899	PRONI
Cavan	1760 abstract	NAI
	1794–1859	Cavan County Archives
Clare	1806–1879 (with gaps)	NAI
	1786–1900	Clare County Library
Cork	1834–1898	Cork City and County Archives
Donegal	1805–1899 (with gaps)	NAI
	1807–1898 (with gaps)	Donegal County Council Archives
Down	1778–1899	PRONI
	1813–1870 (with gaps)	NAI

Dublin	1822–1895	NAI
	1818–1898	Fingal County Archives
Fermanagh	1792–1898 (with gaps)	PRONI
Kerry	1893–1898	NAI
	1874–1889, 1892–1897	Kerry County Archives
Kildare	1844–1860 (Naas barony)	NAI
	1809–1893 (with gaps)	Kildare County Library
Kilkenny	1825–1888 (with gaps)	NAI
	1838–1898	Kilkenny County Library
Laois	1881–1897 (with gaps)	NAI
	1845–1897	Laois County Council Archives
Leitrim	1888 1899 (with gaps)	NAI
Limerick	1888–1899	NAI
	1808–1900	Limerick County Council Archives
Londonderry	1788–1899 (with gaps)	PRONI
Longford	1854–1899	NAI
	1759–1907	Longford County Library
Louth	1851–1892	NAI
	1830–1898	Louth County Library
Mayo	1889–1899	NAI
Meath	1809–1899	NAI
Monaghan	1811–1859	Monaghan County Library
	1798, 1824, 1863/4, 1869, 1890	Clogher Historical Soc.
	1697, 1709	PRONI
Offaly	1892–1897	NAI
	1830–1878	Offaly County Library
Roscommon	1884–1899	NAI
	1818–1899	Roscommon County Council
Sligo	1888–1899	NAI
	1809–1899 (with gaps)	Sligo County Library
Tyrone	1799–1897	PRONI
Waterford	1854+	Waterford County Library
Wicklow	1819–1898	Wicklow County Library

County councils

County councils were established in 1899, superseding the grand juries and taking on many of the functions performed by the boards of guardians. By the early part of the twentieth century there was a steady growth in the influence of the county councils as they acquired housing and planning powers. They were also responsible for elementary and secondary education. The county councils divided the county into districts for the management by a district committee of public heath, housing, roads and water supply.

The most important records for the family historian are the minutes and other records of the council itself and of its committees and the accounts. Local authority records for Northern Ireland are deposited at PRONI and can be located under the reference LA. In the Republic of Ireland the archive departments of local councils hold such records. The Waterford City Archives, for example, hold material originating within Waterford City Council (formerly Waterford Corporation) dating back to the seventeenth century. The principal holdings are:

◆ Minute Books, Waterford Corporation, 1654–1990s (59 volumes)

◆ Committee Records, Waterford Corporation, 1778–1940s (19 committees)

◆ Records of Town Clerk's Office, 1700–1990s

◆ Records of Finance Office, 1796–1980s

◆ Records of City Engineer's Office, 1700–1990s including over 2500 maps, plans and drawings for the city and its environs from the eighteenth century to the present. There are also many reports and photographs of completed and proposed works.

For more details see www.waterfordcity.ie/archives.htm

Fingal County Archives (Dublin County Council records) hold material relating to the former Dublin City Council and its predecessor bodies, including boards of guardians and grand juries. These are also the records of the Rural District Councils of Balrothery, Dublin North, Dublin South and Rathdown and the Rural District Council of Celbridge. See www.iol.ie/~fincolib/archives.htm.

Cork City Archives hold an extensive collection of local authority records including those of various poor law unions, corporations, the Rural District Councils of Bandon, Bantry, Castletown, Clonakilty, Cork, Dunmanway, Kinsale, Macroom, Schull and Youghal and the Urban District Councils of Clonakilty and Youghal. See www.corkcity.ie/facilities/archives_larecords.html.

The best guide to the local authority collections held in Ireland is the *Directory of Irish Archives*, by Seamus Helferty and Raymond Refausse. Also see the *Guide to Local Authority Archives in Ireland*, produced by the Local Authority Archivists Group, published in 2004.

19 Researching Online

F AMILY HISTORY IS SAID TO BE the second most researched topic on the Internet (I'll let you guess the most popular!) and any search engine will produce hundreds or even thousands of entries if you type in 'genealogy'. The resources that are available on the Internet are increasing on a daily basis. Online sites can prove particularly useful to the beginner who wishes to find out what is available and where the information is held. Many sites highlight the main categories of records and provide useful guidance and support. The Internet also enables researchers to get in touch with others holding similar interests through the speed and convenience of e-mail.

It is important to remember that the Internet is not yet a replacement for any of the other important resources available to the family historian, particularly archives, libraries and the local LDS Family History Centre. The General Register Office of Ireland, for example, provides information online as to what is contained in its archives, but does not give digital access to this information. The NAI, NLI and PRONI websites also provide details of what genealogical information is held in their archives, but require researchers to either visit the archive or pay a professional researcher to do so on their behalf.

Although more and more research is now being carried out online, it is also important to be aware of the dangers and pitfalls that are associated with obtaining information in this way. Uploaded family-tree information can contain misspellings and inaccurate dates and locations. More frustratingly, the information is often not properly attributed and, therefore, researchers must simply trust that the information is correct. The only sure way to know that the information you find is accurate and genuine is by locating the document in the relevant archive and reading it yourself!

Another frequent problem can be found with common surnames. If you have a popular surname and carry out Internet searches, you may waste valuable time following false leads.

Nevertheless, it would be foolish not to utilize the thousands of Irish family history websites now available. Google, Yahoo and Alta Vista are just a few of the powerful search engines which will allow you to find whatever you are looking for anywhere in the world. Simply type in your ancestor's surname, first name and a location (the more precise the better) and you may be surprised at the number of matches you can find.

Message boards and mailing lists

The best way to ask others for help with your family history is to post a query on a popular genealogical message board. This is a great method of getting in touch with others at home and aboard who may have information which is relevant to your research. Simply put a name, date range, and place in a message title, like this: 'Richard Maxwell, born 1871, County Armagh'. In the body of your message, be concise while providing enough detail so that others will find your message. It is then a matter of waiting for others to respond.

You can also join a mailing list. A mailing list is simply an e-mail party line: every message that a list subscriber sends to the list is distributed to all other list subscribers. Subscribing to a mailing list is one way of connecting to people who share your interests. If you do not find a mailing list covering your topic of interest, you can always start one.

The best sites include:

RootsWeb.com – searches.rootsweb.com/share.html

The primary purpose and function of RootsWeb.com is to connect people so that they can help each other and share genealogical research. Most resources on RootsWeb.com are designed to facilitate such connections. There are more than 132,000 message boards related to surnames, localities, and other topics. By posting a message to the appropriate message board, you create a record through which other researchers can find you. If you do not find a message board covering your topic of interest, start one.

Ancestry.com – www.ancestry.myfamily.com/trees/awt/main.aspx

The Ancestry World Tree contains nearly 400 million names in family trees submitted by our users. The Ancestry World Tree is the largest collection of its kind on the Internet.

Genes Reunited – www.genesreunited.co.uk

This site can help you to find people whose ancestors match your own. Without a subscription you can upload a pedigree and be contacted by others, but you need to subscribe in order to initiate contacts yourself.

A list of available Ireland mailing lists can be found on John Fuller's website, *Genealogy Resources on the Internet*, www.rootsweb.com/~jfuller/gen_mail_country-unk-irl.html.

General sites

A number of websites exist which have searchable databases containing a billion or so names. At the other end of the spectrum there are thousands of personal websites put up by keen individuals and groups, reflecting their family histories.

The most interesting general websites include:

Cyndi's List – Ireland and Northern Ireland – www.cyndislist.com/ireland.htm

Cyndi's List is the largest directory of genealogy and family history on the Internet. The huge section on Ireland and Northern Ireland contains links to hundreds of websites that specialize in Irish family history and is a great place for the inexperienced researcher to begin.

Genealogy.com – www.genealogy.com

Genealogy.com offers a wide range of searchable data for a fee. Major Irish collections include:

- ◆ Irish and British Immigrants to America
- ◆ 1860s–1870s Passenger and Immigration Lists
- ◆ an Index to Griffith's Valuation of Ireland
- ◆ the Irish Flax Grower's List, 1796
- ◆ Tithe Applotment Books of Ireland

FamilySearch – www.familysearch.com

The Family History Library of the Genealogy Society of Utah (GSU) in Salt Lake City, USA has a website that is accessed daily by millions of people around the world. It contains over a billion records and an online catalogue of the largest Irish genealogy collection available anywhere in the world.

RootsWeb.com – www.rootsweb.com

RootsWeb.com describes itself as the oldest and largest free genealogical community in the world. It runs a surname listing of some 750,000 names drawn mainly from civil registration sources for England and Wales. Among its user-submitted databases, RootsWeb includes some death records for Co. Tipperary at www.userdb.rootsweb.com/regional.html.Irl.

Ancestry.com – www.Ancestry.com

Ancestry.com holds the largest collection of family history records on the Internet, with over 2 billion names. Although mainly US-based, some of its databases come from Irish records and others contain information on Irish immigrants arriving in America. Ancestry.com also offers *Family Tree Makers*, the best-selling genealogy program in the world, which can automatically search databases on Ancestry.com.

GENUKI – www.genuki.co.uk

GENUKI acts as a virtual reference library of genealogical sources for the UK and Ireland and is maintained by a group of experts who are responsible for creating and maintaining research toolkits and access to online news-groups. GENUKI provides a comprehensive list of records available for every county in Ireland.

American Family Immigration History Centre – www.ellisisland.org

For many Irish immigrants beginning a new life in America, Ellis Island was their first experience of life across the Atlantic. The Church of the Latter-Day Saints (LDS) indexed the names of all Ellis Island immigrants from microfilms of the original passenger lists, and these are now part of a computer database. Once you have located your immigrant ancestor, you can view the original ship's manifest and discover your ancestor's birthplace, occupation, height, eye colour, and cash on hand when disembarking at the port of New York.

Irish websites

The best Irish websites will help pinpoint what information is available for each county and where the records are located. Many have information gathered from census records and other records which are freely available to researchers. The best of these sites are:

IrelandGenWeb Project – www.irelandgenweb.com

The IrelandGenWeb Project is part of WorldGenWeb, supported by volunteers who are attempting to build communities of family historians all around the world dedicated to local genealogical research. It consists of county websites which feature genealogical databases, research guides, and useful links.

Irish Genealogy – www.irishgenealogy.ie

Irish Genealogy allows you to search indexes of computerized records from many Heritage Centres derived from about 15 million religious, civil and land records dating as far back as the seventeenth century. Eleven counties in Ireland are currently represented: Armagh, Cavan, Derry, Donegal, Fermanagh, Leitrim, Limerick, Mayo, Sligo, Tyrone and Wexford. More counties will be added over time. To see complete details of these records, you can request the information for a fee from the relevant Heritage Centre (see p. 183).

Irish Origins – www.irishorigins.com

Irish Origins offers many valuable collections of Irish genealogical material online, including Griffith's Valuation, Griffith's survey maps, an 1851 census of Dublin City, Tithe Defaulters, 1831, an index of Irish wills pre-1858 and other databases for Irish genealogists. As a subscriber you can search and view collections in full.

Eneclann – www.eneclann.ie

Eneclann is the largest family history research firm in Ireland. It is involved in a number of unique digitization and indexing projects at major archives and libraries in Ireland. A number of record collections digitized by Eneclann are searchable for a fee on Irish Origins.

Fianna Guide to Irish Genealogy – www.rootsweb.com/~fianna/county/index.html

Fianna has produced a comprehensive website which contains details of sources available for every county in Ireland including lists of church records A great deal of invaluable information is available online, such as details of records held for each county, details of civil and Roman Catholic parishes and local research facilities. Extensive transcripts are available online for some counties, including muster rolls, freeholders lists and marriage and census extracts.

Irish Ancestors – www.ireland.com/ancestor/index.htm

John Grenham and the *Irish Times* have produced an online genealogy guide based on Grenham's 1992 book *Tracing Your Irish Ancestors*. Although this is a subscription site, it has a lot of free information to help you get started on Irish family history, including a database of more than 65,000 Irish place names to pinpoint your county and parish.

Archives

FamilyRecords – www.familyrecords.gov.uk/partners.htm

The FamilyRecords portal is run by a consortium including the National Archives, London, PRONI, National Archives of Scotland, the Family Records Centre, the Imperial War Museum, the National Library of Wales, the General Register Office (for England and Wales), the General Register Office for Scotland and the British Library India Office. It provides links to the websites of these bodies and to official information.

National Archives, London – www.pro.gov.uk

The National Archives runs a very substantial website that refers to records that can be consulted at Kew or the Family Records Centre in Islington. There is definitive information on tracing ancestors in the armed forces (particularly useful for those with Irish ancestors who served in the British Army) while research guides provide detailed information about specific historical records.

Public Record Office of Northern Ireland (PRONI) – proni.nics.gov.uk/index.htm

PRONI is the major repository of public records in Northern Ireland. PRONI holds millions of documents that relate chiefly, but by no means exclusively, to present-day Northern Ireland. The earliest record dates from 1219, with the main concentration of records covering the period 1600 to the present.

General Register Office (Oifig An Ard-Chlaraitheora) – www.groireland.ie

This is the main repository in the Republic of Ireland for birth, death and marriage records for the Republic. Holdings include registers of all births registered in the whole of Ireland from 1 January 1864 to 31 December 1921, all deaths registered in the whole of Ireland from 1 January 1864 to 31 December 1921, and in the Republic from that date, and all marriages registered in the whole of Ireland from 1 April 1845 to 31 December 1863, except those celebrated by the Roman Catholic clergy.

General Register Office of Northern Ireland (GRO) – www.groni.gov.uk/index.htm

The GRO is responsible for the administration of marriage law and the provision of a system for the civil registration of births, deaths, marriages and adoptions in Northern Ireland. Birth and death registers are available from 1 January 1864. Marriage registers are available only for marriages on and after 1 January 1922. District registrars' offices across Northern Ireland hold marriage registers dating from 1 April 1845 for non Roman Catholic marriages and from 1 January 1864 for all marriages. It is possible to order birth certificates, etc., online.

National Archives of Ireland – www.nationalarchives.ie

This site provides useful guides to many of the NAI's collections, including census returns, tithe applotment books, Griffith's Valuation, wills and testamentary records. With the exception of the Ireland–Australian transportation database (1791–1853) the records themselves are not searchable on this site and must be consulted in the Search Room.

National Library of Ireland – www.nli.ie/

The holdings include microfilms of Catholic parish registers, copies of the important nineteenth-century land valuations (the tithe applotment books and Griffith's Valuation), trade and social directories, estate records and newspapers.

Familia – www.familia.org.uk/about.html

Familia is a web-based directory of family history resources held in public libraries in the UK and Ireland and is the online starting-place to find information about materials in public libraries which will help you trace your family history.

Societies

Society of Genealogists – www.sog.org.uk

The Society of Genealogists offers a unique combination of research material, guidance and support for those interested in family history with its useful bookshop and a collection which includes indexes to Griffith's Valuation (1848–64), tithe applotment books (1823–38), Armagh Prerogative Court wills (1530–1858), Registry of Deeds wills (1708–1832) and other indexes of Irish wills up to 1858, memorials of the dead in Ireland (tombstone inscriptions) and Dublin directories 1761–1846.

Federation of Family History Societies – www.ffhs.org.uk

The Federation of Family History Societies provides a useful overview and links with local societies.

Irish Genealogical Research Society – www.igrsoc.org/

The IGRS was established in 1936 in London to encourage and promote the study of Irish genealogy and to collect books and manuscripts of genealogical value. Membership benefits include access to the largest private library of Irish genealogical material in Britain and receipt of the journal *The Irish Genealogist* (produced annually) and the bi-annual newsletter.

Irish Family History Society – homepage.eircom.net/~ifhs/IFHShome.htm

The society aims to promote the study of Irish family history and genealogy. Its site includes useful links and a membership forum.

North of Ireland Family History Society – www.nifhs.org/

This society, established in 1979, consists of ten family history societies in Northern Ireland and has now hundreds of members worldwide. It publishes the journal *North Irish Roots* twice a year, providing a means for members to communicate their interests to others.

Genealogical Society of Ireland – www.familyhistory.ie/

The Genealogical Society of Ireland was established to promote an interest in genealogy in Ireland by organizing open meetings, lectures, workshops and publishing genealogical material.

Useful Research Resources

Major Irish repositories

BELFAST CENTRAL LIBRARY

Royal Avenue, Belfast BT1 1EA, Northern Ireland
Telephone: +44 (0) 28 9050 9150
Fax: +44 (0) 28 9033 2819
E-mail: info@libraries.belfast-elb.gov.uk
Website: www.belb.org.uk

The collection includes some 1,000,000 volumes, plus the largest
newspaper collection in Northern Ireland. In addition, the library
maintains significant collections of periodicals, maps, microfilms,
music scores, pamphlets, photographs, postcards, music recordings,
theatre materials and government documents for Northern Ireland,
the Republic of Ireland and the UK. The library does not offer
genealogical services per se, but its holdings in this area are extensive,
and staff are willing to assist researchers as far as possible.

The General Register Office (Oifig An Ard-Chlaraitheora)

Joyce House, 8/11 Lombard Street, Dublin 2, Ireland
Telephone: +353 (0) 90 6632900
Fax: +353 (0) 90 6632999
E-mail by submission form at www.groireland.ie/contact_details.htm
Website: www.groireland.ie/

This is the civil repository for records relating to births, death and marriages in the Republic of Ireland. The archive includes registers of all births and deaths registered in Ireland from 1 January 1864 to 31 December 1921, registers of all marriages registered in Ireland from 1 April 1845 to 31 December 1863 except those celebrated by the Roman Catholic clergy, and registers of all marriages registered in the whole of Ireland from 1 January 1864 to 31 December 1921.

GENERAL REGISTER OFFICE, BELFAST

Northern Ireland Statistics and Research Agency, Oxford House, 49/55 Chichester Street, Belfast BT1 4HL, Northern Ireland
Telephone: +44 (0) 28 9025 2000
Fax: +44 (0) 28 9025 2044
E-mail: gro.nistra@dfpni.gov.uk (birth, death and marriage certificate enquiries)
E-mail: groreg.nistra@dfpni.gov.uk (marriage, re-registration and adoptions)
E-mail: grostats.nistra@dfpni.gov.uk (statistical queries)
Website: www.groni.gov.uk

The GRO, formally established in 1922 following Partition, stores vital records of Northern Ireland for issue of certified copies to the public. Birth, death and Roman Catholic marriage registrations date from 1864 to present; non-Roman Catholic marriages from 1845 to present; adoptions from 1930 to present; and still-births from 1961 to present.

LINEN HALL LIBRARY

17 Donegall Square North, Belfast BT1 5GD, Northern Ireland
Telephone: +44 (0) 28 9032 1707
Fax: +44 (0) 28 9043 8586
E-mail: info@linenhall.com
Website: www.linenhall.com/Home/home.html

The library houses more than 250,000 volumes, 75,000 pamphlets, plus significant holdings of periodicals, newspapers, manuscripts, maps, microfilms, photographs, films and recordings. It maintains a general lending and reference collection, the latter being especially strong in genealogy, heraldry, history and travel. Its great strength, however, is its Irish and local studies collection, with particular emphasis on Belfast and Counties Antrim and Down.

NATIONAL ARCHIVES OF IRELAND

Bishop Street, Dublin 8, Ireland
Telephone: +353 (0) 1 407 2300
Fax: +353 (0) 1 407 2333
E-mail: mail@nationalarchives.ie
Website: www.nationalarchives.ie

The NAI was formally established in 1988 with the amalgamation of the Public Record Office of Ireland and the State Paper Office. It is the official depository for the records of the Irish government. Amongst the most consulted records are Census 1901; Census 1911; Cholera Papers (Board of Health); Customs and Excise; Famine Relief Commission; National School applications, registers and files; Valuation Office and Boundary Survey records.

NATIONAL LIBRARY OF IRELAND

Kildare Street, Dublin 2, Ireland
Telephone: +353 (0) 1 603 0200
Fax: +353 (0) 1 676 6690
E-mail: info@nli.ie
Website: www.nli.ie

The NLI is Ireland's major public research library, established 'to collect, preserve and make accessible materials on or relating to Ireland, whether published in Ireland or abroad, and a supporting reference collection'. To this end it seeks to build a comprehensive collection documenting the history, culture and life of Ireland. The library houses a collection of some 1,000,000 printed books, including pamphlets; approximately 17,000 linear feet of manuscripts; some 150,000 maps, in either print or manuscript form; about 2500 current periodical titles; around 10,000 reels of microfilms; 300 current newspaper titles, plus complete files of many non-current titles; about 630,000 photographs, which are held in the library's National Photographic Archive; and some 90,000 prints and drawings, including significant holdings of architectural records.

OFFICE OF THE CHIEF HERALD/GENEALOGICAL OFFICE

2–3 Kildare Street, Dublin 2, Ireland
Telephone: +353 (0) 1603 0230
Fax: +353 (0) 1662 1061
E-mail: herald@nli.ie
Website: www.nli.ie

Founded as the Office of the Ulster King of Arms in 1552, the Office of the Chief Herald is the oldest office of State in Ireland. The Chief Herald is the Heraldic Authority for Ireland, responsible for the regulation of heraldic matters and the granting and confirming of coats of arms. Documents deriving from the functions of the office include the registers of the Chief Herald, armorials and ordinaries of arms, funeral entries, lords' entries and records of knights dubbed. Roger O'Ferrall's *Linea Antiqua* is the most important source for ancient genealogies of Gaelic families and also contains exemplifications of arms.

PRESBYTERIAN HISTORICAL SOCIETY

Room 218, Church House, Fisherwick Place, Belfast BT1 6DW,
     Northern Ireland
Telephone: +44 (0) 28 9032 2284

The Presbyterian Historical Society was created in 1906 to promote public awareness of the history of the Presbyterian Churches in Ireland. It is largely supported by the Presbyterian Church in Ireland. The society possesses a library of some 12,000 books and pamphlets. These are mainly concerned with ecclesiastical history and in particular Presbyterian history. The collection includes a large number of congregational histories. Manuscript material includes session minutes, baptisms and marriages from individual churches as well as some presbytery minutes.

PUBLIC RECORD OFFICE OF NORTHERN IRELAND

66 Balmoral Avenue, Belfast BT9 6NY, Northern Ireland
Telephone: +44 (0) 28 9025138
Fax: +44 (0) 289025 5999
E-mail: proni@gov.uk
Website: www.proni.gov.uk

PRONI was established in 1923 following Partition and opened
in 1924 as the official repository for public records in Northern
Ireland, but it also houses the largest collection of private records
in Northern Ireland. Records fall into three major categories:
records of government departments, some going back to the early
nineteenth century; records of courts of law, local authorities and
non-departmental public bodies; and records deposited by private
individuals, estates, churches, business and institutions.

REGISTRY OF DEEDS

Henrietta Street, Dublin 1, Ireland
Telephone: +353 (0) 1 670 7500
Fax: +353 (0) 1 804 8406
Website: www.irlgov.ie/landreg

Documents retained in the Registry of Deeds include: memorials
(1708 to present, microfilmed 1930 to present), transcripts (1708–
1960 with some gaps), abstracts (1833–1969), names index or index
of grantors, and lands index (1708–1946).

REPRESENTATIVE CHURCH BODY LIBRARY

Braemor Park, Churchtown, Dublin 14, Ireland
Telephone: +353 (0) 1 492 3979
Fax: +353 (0) 1 492 4770
E-mail: library@ireland.anglican.org
Website: www.ireland.anglican.org

This library was founded in 1931 and has been developed as the
theological and reference library of the Church of Ireland and as
the Church's principal repository for its archives and manuscripts.

The library houses some 40,000 volumes, focusing on theology and history, plus architectural records, archives and manuscripts, microfilms, pamphlets, photographs, and recordings. Major archival collections include: Church of Ireland archives chiefly for the Republic of Ireland, representing more than 700 parishes, mainly in Counties Carlow, Clare, Cork, Dublin, Galway, Kerry, Kildare, Kilkenny, Mayo, Meath, Westmeath, and Wicklow; the records of 17 dioceses; and the records of 15 cathedrals, especially Christ Church and St Patrick's in Dublin, St Canice's in Kilkenny, and St Brigid's in Kildare.

Societies

REPUBLIC OF IRELAND

Irish Family History Society
Post Office Box 36, Naas, Co. Kildare, Ireland
Website: http://homepage.eircom.net/~ifhs/

The Irish Family History Society promotes the study of Irish family history and genealogy through its journal, which contains aids to genealogical research, details of current research and articles. It was also publishes a *Members Interest Directory* annually and an occasional newssheet containing up-to-date information on the society's activities, members' queries and details of future lecturers, seminars and workshops.

Irish Family History Society Ballinteer Branch
29 The View, Woodpark, Ballinteer, Dundrum, Dublin 16, Ireland
E-mail: ryanc@iol.ie

Irish Genealogical Research Society
14 Ascaill Ghairbhile, Ráth Garbh, Dublin, Ireland

Genealogical Society of Ireland
(formerly the Dun Laoghaire Genealogical Society)
14 Rochestown Park, Dun Laoghaire, Co. Dublin, Ireland
E-mail: dlgs@iol.ie
Website: www.dun-laoghaire.com/genealogy

Cork Genealogical Society
4 Evergreen Villas, Evergreen Road, Cork City, Ireland
Website: http://homepage.eircom.net/~aocoleman/

County Roscommon Family History Society
(formerly Irish Connections Family History Research Group and
    Society)
Bealnamullia, Athlone, County Roscommon, Ireland

Wexford Family History Society
24 Parklands, Wexford, Co. Wexford, Ireland

NORTHERN IRELAND

North of Ireland Family History Society
c/o Queen's University, Dept. of Education, Belfast BT7 1HL,
    Northern Ireland
Website: www.nifhs.org

This society, established in 1979, consists of ten family history
societies in Northern Ireland and has now hundreds of members
worldwide. The objective of the society is to foster an interest in
family history with special reference to families who have roots in
Northern Ireland. It publishes a journal, *North Irish Roots*, twice a year,
providing a means for members to communicate their interests to
others.

Ulster Historical and Genealogical Guild
Ulster Historical Foundation, 12 College Square East,
Belfast BT1 6DD, Northern Ireland
E-mail: enquiry@uhf.org.uk
Website: www.uhf.org.uk

The Guild is essentially a research co-operative and has a membership
register past the 12,000 mark. Its aims are to prevent duplication of
research effort and to bring together people with similar interests.
Members receive two annual publications: *Familia: Ulster Genealogical
Review*, which contains articles on Irish history and genealogy, and the
Directory of Irish Family History Research, which is the most complete
and up-to-date record of Irish genealogical research in progress

enabling family historians world-wide to publicize their research interests.

SOCIETIES ABROAD

AUSTRALIA

Irish Interest Group, Society of Australian Genealogists
Richmond Villa, 120 Kent Street, Sydney NSW 2000, Australia
Website: www.sag.org.au/sigs.htm

CANADA

Irish Interest Group, Alberta Family Histories Society
PO Box 30270, Station B, Calgary, Alberta, T2M 4P1, Canada
Website: www.calcna.ab.ca/afhs/sigs.html

Ottawa Branch, Ontario Genealogical Society
PO Box 8346, Ottawa, Ontario K1G 3H8, Canada
E-mail: ogsottawa@cyberus.ca
Website: www.calcna.ab.ca/afhs/sigs.html

British Isles Family History Society of Greater Ottawa
PO Box 38026, Ottawa, ON K2C 1N0, Canada
Telephone: (613) 224 9868
Website: www.cyberus.ca/~bifhsgo

ENGLAND

Irish Genealogical Research Society
82 Eaton Square, London SW1W 9AJ, England

NEW ZEALAND

Irish Interest Group, New Zealand Society of Genealogists
P O Box 8795, Symonds Street, Auckland 1035, New Zealand
Website: www.genealogy.org.nz/Branches/branches_frame.html

UNITED STATES

International Society for British Genealogy and Family History
PO Box 3115, Salt Lake City, UT 84110-3115, USA

Irish Genealogical Society of Michigan
5237 Folkestone Drive, Troy, MI 48098-3222, USA

British Isles Genealogical Society of Wisconsin and Illinois
1012 Rene Court, Park Ridge, IL 60068, USA

Irish Genealogical Society of Wisconsin
PO Box 13766, Wauwatosa, WI 53213-0766, USA
Website: www.execpc.com/~igsw/

British Isles Family History Society – USA
2531 Sawtelle Blvd. #134, Los Angeles, CA 90064-3163, USA
Website: www.rootsweb.com/~bifhsusa/

The Irish Ancestral Research Association (TIARA)
PO Box 619, Sudbury, MA 01776, USA
Website: http://world.std.com/~ahern/TIARA.html

Irish Genealogical Society International
PO Box 16585, St Paul, MN 55116, USA
Website: www.rootsweb.com/~irish/

Irish Family History Forum
PO Box 67, Plainview, NY 11803, USA

British Isles Genealogical Research Association
PO Box 19775, San Diego, CA 92159-0775, USA

Family History Centres in Ireland

CORK

Sarsfield Road, Wilton, Cork, Co. Cork, Ireland
Telephone: +353 (0) 21-4897050
Hours: T 10am–12 noon; W 7–9pm

DUBLIN

Finglas Road, Glasnevin, Dublin 9, Ireland
Hours: T 4–9pm, Th 10am–2pm, 6–9pm

LIMERICK

Doradoyle Road, Limerick, Co. Limerick, Ireland
Hours: F 7–9pm

BELFAST

403 Holywood Road, Belfast BT14 2GU, Northern Ireland
Telephone: +44 (0) 28-9076 9839
Hours: W, Th 10am–4pm; Sat 9am–1pm; T–Th 7–9.30pm (LDS members only); F 10am–1pm (LDS members only)

COLERAINE

8 Sandelfield, Knocklynn Road, Coleraine,
    Co. Londonderry BT52 1WQ, Northern Ireland
Telephone: +44 (0) 2870-321214
Hours: T 9.30am–2.30pm; W 6.30–8.30pm

LONDONDERRY

Racecourse Road, Belmont Estate, Londonderry,
    Co. Londonderry BT48, Northern Ireland
Telephone: +44 (0) 28–7135 0179
Hours: M, W, Th 10am–2pm; Th 7–9pm

County Heritage Centres

Established as part of the Irish Genealogical Project, whose aim is to create a comprehensive genealogical database for the entire island of Ireland, each centre indexes and computerizes records of a particular county, or in some cases two counties. Staff will search their databases for a fee. If you know only the name of the county your ancestor came from, one of these centres may be the best way of finding a more specific place of origin.

ANTRIM

Ulster Historical Foundation
Balmoral Buildings, 12 College Square East, Belfast BTI 6DD
Telephone: +44 (0) 2890–332288
Fax: +44 (0) 2890–239885
Website: www.uhf.org.uk

ARMAGH

Armagh Ancestry
42 English St, Armagh BT61 7AB
Telephone: +44 (0) 2837-521802
Fax: +44 (0) 2837-510033
Website: www.irishroots.net/Armagh.htm

CARLOW

Carlow Genealogy
Carlow County Council, Carlow Town, Co. Carlow
Telephone/Fax: + 353 (0) 503-30850
Website: www.irishroots.net/Carlow.htm

CAVAN

Cavan Genealogical Research Centre
Cana House, Farnham St, Cavan Town, Co. Cavan
Telephone: + 353 (0) 49-4361094
Fax: + 353 (0) 49-4331494
Website: www.irishroots.net/Cavan.htm

CLARE

Clare Heritage and Genealogical Centre
Church St, Coro fin, Co. Clare
Telephone: + 353 (0) 65-6837955
Fax: + 353 (0) 65-6837540
Website: clare.irishroots.net/

CORK

Cork Ancestry
c/o County Library, Farranlea Rd, Cork City
Telephone: + 353 (0) 21-4346435
Website: www.irishroots.net/Cork.htm

Mallow Heritage Centre
27–28 Bank Place, Mallow, Co. Cork
Telephone: + 353 (0) 22-50302
Fax: + 353 (0) 22-20276
Website: www.irishroots.net/Cork.htm

LONDONDERRY/DERRY

Heritage Library
14 Bishop St, Derry City, Co. Londonderry BT48 6PW
Telephone: + 44 (0) 28 71269792/71361661
Fax: + 44 (0) 28 71360921
E-mail: niancestors@btclick.com

DOWN

Ulster Historical Foundation
Balmoral Buildings, 12 College Square East, Belfast BTI 6DD
Telephone: +44 (0) 2890-332288
Fax: +44 (0) 2890-239885
Website: www.uhf.org.uk

Banbridge Genealogy Services
c/o Banbridge Gateway Tourist Information Centre,
    200 Newry Road, Banbridge, Co. Down BT32 3NB
Telephone: +44 (0) 2840-626369
Fax: +44 (0) 2840-623114
Website: www.banbridge.com

DONEGAL

Donegal Ancestry Ltd
Old Meeting House, Back Lane, Ramelton, Co. Donegal
Telephone/Fax: + 353 (0) 74-51266
Website: www.irishroots.net/Donegal.htm

DUBLIN

Dun Laoghaire Borough Heritage Society
Moran Park House, Dun Laoghaire, Co. Dublin
Telephone: + 353 (0) 1-2054700
Website: www.irishroots.net/Dublin.htm

Fingal Heritage Group
Carnegie Library, North St, Swords, Co. Dublin
Telephone/Fax: + 353 (0) 1-8400080
Website: www.irishroots.net/Dublin.htm

FERMANAGH

Heritage World
The Heritage Centre, 26 Market Square, Dungannon,
    Co. Tyrone BT70 1AB
Telephone: +44 (0) 2887-724187
Fax: +44 (0) 2887-752141
Website: www.irishroots.net/FnghTyrn.htm

Irish World
Donoughmore Heritage Centre, Donoughmore Old School,
    Pomeroy Road, Donoughmore, Co. Tyrone
Telephone/Fax: +44 (0) 2887-767039

GALWAY

East Galway Family History Society Co. Ltd
Woodford, Loughrea, Co. Galway
Telephone: + 353 (0) 509-49309
Fax: + 353 (0) 509-49546
Website:www.irishroots.net/Galway.htm

West Galway Family History Society
Unit 3, Liosbaun Estate, Tuam Road, Galway City
Telephone: + 353 (0) 91-756737
Website: www.irishroots.net/Galway.htm

KILDARE

Kildare Heritage Project
c/o Kildare County Library, Newbridge, Co. Kildare
Telephone: + 353 (0) 45-433602
Fax: + 353 (0) 45-432490
Website: www.irishroots.net/Kildare.htm

KILKENNY

Kilkenny Ancestry
Rothe House, Parliament St, Kilkenny City
Telephone/Fax: + 353 (0) 56-22893
Website: www.irishroots.net/Kilknny.htm

LEITRIM

Leitrim Heritage Centre
County Library, Ballinamore, Co. Leitrim
Telephone: + 353 (0) 78-44012
Fax: + 353 (0) 78-44425
Website: www.irishroots.net/Leitrim.htm

LIMERICK

Limerick Ancestry
The Granary, Michael St, Limerick City
Telephone: + 353 (0) 61-415125/312988
Fax: + 353 (0) 61-321985
Website: www.irishroots.net/Limerick.htm

LONGFORD

Longford Roots
Longford Museum and Heritage Centre, 1 Church St,
    Longford Town, Co. Longford
Telephone: + 353 (0) 43-41235
Fax: + 353 (0) 43-41279
Website: www.irishroots.net/Longford.htm

LOUTH

Louth County Library
Roden Place, Dundalk
Telephone: + 353 (0) 42-9353190
Website: www.louthcoco.ie

LAOIS

Laois and Offaly Family History Research Centre
Bury Quay, Tullamore, Co. Offaly
Telephone/Fax: + 353 (0) 506-21421
Website: www.irishmidlandsancestry.com

MAYO

Mayo North Family Heritage
Eniscoe, Castle Hill, Ballina, Co. Mayo
Telephone: + 353 (0) 96-31809
Fax: + 353 (0) 96-31885
Website: mayo.irish-roots.net/

South Mayo Family Research Centre
Ballinrobe, Co. Mayo
Telephone/Fax: + 353 (0) 92-41214

Meath Heritage Centre
Mill Street, Trim, Co. Meath
Telephone: + 353 (0) 46-36633
Fax: + 353 (0) 46-37502
Website: www.irishroots.net/meath.htm

MONAGHAN

Monaghan Ancestry
Clogher Historical Society, 6 Tully St, Monaghan Town,
    Co. Monaghan
Website: www.irishroots.net/Monaghan.htm

OFFALY

Laois and Offaly Family History Research Centre
Bury Quay, Tullamore, Co. Offaly
Telephone/Fax: + 353 (0) 506-21421
Website: www.irishmidlandsancestry.com

ROSCOMMON

Co. Roscommon Heritage and Genealogical Society
Church St. Strokestown, Co. Roscommon
Telephone: + 353 (0) 78-33390
Fax: + 353 (0) 78-33398
Website: www.irishroots.net/Roscmmn.htm

SLIGO

Co. Sligo Heritage and Genealogical Society
Aras Reddan, Temple St, Sligo Town
Telephone: + 353 (0) 71-43728
Website: www.irishroots.net/Sligo.htm

TIPPERARY

Tipperary North Family Research Centre
The Gatehouse, Kickham St, Nenagh, Co. Tipperary
Telephone: + 353 (0) 67-33850
Fax: + 353 (0) 67-33586
Website: www.irishroots.net/Tipp.htm

Roscrea Heritage Centre
(research service for Roscrea and surrounding parishes)
GPA Damer House, Castle St, Roscrea, Co. Tipperary
Telephone: + 353 (0) 505-21850

Tipperary Family History Research
Excel Heritage Centre, Mitchell St, Tipperary Town, Co. Tipperary
Telephone: + 353 (0) 62-80555/80556
Fax: + 353 (0) 62-80551
Website: www.tfhr.org

Tipperary South
Brú Ború Heritage Centre, Rock of Cashel, Co. Tipperary
Telephone: + 353 (0) 62-61122
Fax: + 353 (0) 62-62700
Website: www.irishroots.net/Tipp.htm

TYRONE

Heritage World
The Heritage Centre, 26 Market Square, Dungannon,
    Co. Tyrone BT70 1AB
Telephone: +44 (0) 2887-724187
Fax: +44 (0) 2887-752141
Website: www.heritagewld.com

WATERFORD

Waterford Heritage Centre
St Patrick's Church, Jenkin's Lane, Waterford City
Telephone: + 353 (0) 51- 876123
Fax: + 353 (0) 51-850645
Website: www.irishroots.net/Waterford.htm

WESTMEATH

Dun na Sí,
Heritage Centre, Knockdomney, Moate, Co. Westmeath
Telephone: + 353 (0) 902-81183
Fax: + 353 (0) 902-81661
Website: www.irishroots.net/Wstmeath.htm

WEXFORD

County Wexford Heritage and Genealogical Society
Yola Farmstead, Tagoat, Co. Wexford
Telephone/Fax: + 353 (0) 53-31177
Website: www.irishroots.net/Wexford.htm

WICKLOW

Co. Wicklow Family History Centre
Wicklow's Historic Gaol, Kilmantin Hill, Wicklow Town
Telephone: + 353 (0) 404-20126
Fax: + 353 (0) 404-61612
Website: www.wicklow.ie

Reference books

BARDON, J. *A History of Ulster* (Belfast, 1992)
BARNARD, T. *A Guide to Sources for the History of Material Culture in Ireland, 1500–2000* (Four Courts Press, 2005)
BARTLETT, T. and JEFFREY, K. (eds) *A Military History of Ireland* (Cambridge, 1996)
BEGLEY, D.F. (ed) *Irish Genealogy: A Record Finder* (Dublin, 1981)
CARLETON, S.T. *Heads and Hearths: the Hearth Money Rolls and Poll Tax Returns for Co. Antrim, 1660–69* (Belfast, 1991)
CHRISTIAN, P. *The Genealogist's Internet* (National Archives, London, 2001)
CLARE, Rev. W. *A Simple Guide to Irish Genealogy* (London, 1938)
CONNOLLY, S.J. (ed) *The Oxford Companion To Irish History* (Oxford, 1998)
CRAWFORD, W.H. 'The Significance of Landed Estates in Ulster 1600–1820', in *Irish Economic and Social History, XVII* (1990)

CRAWFORD, W.H. 'The Ulster Irish in the Eighteenth Century', in *Ulster Folklife*, vol. 28, 1982

CRAWFORD, W.H., and TRAINOR, B. *Aspects of Irish Social History, 1750–1800* (Belfast, 1969)

DE BREFFNY, B. *Irish Family Names: Arms, Origins and Locations* (Dublin, 1982)

DICKSON, R.J. *Ulster Emigration to Colonial America 1718–1775* (Belfast, 1966)

DOOLEY, T. *Sources for the History of Landed Estates in Ireland* (Dublin, 2000)

FABRICANT, C. *Swift's Landscape* (Johns Hopkins University Press, London, 1982)

FALLEY, M.D. *Irish and Scotch-Irish Ancestral Research* (Virginia, 1962)

GILLESPIE, R.G. (ed) *Settlement and Survival On an Ulster Estate* (Belfast, 1988)

GREEN, E.R.R. (ed) *Essays in Scotch-Irish History*, (Belfast, 1969)

GRENHAM, J. *Tracing Your Irish Ancestors* (Dublin, 1992)

HAYWARD, R. *In Praise of Ulster* (Belfast, 1938)

HELFERTY, S. and REFAUSSE R. *A Directory of Irish Archives*, 4th edn (Dublin, 2003)

HERBER, M.D. *Ancestor Trails: The Complete Guide to British Genealogy and Family History* (Sutton Publishing, 1997)

HEY, D. *The Oxford Companion to Local and Family History* (Oxford, 1996)

HOWELLS, C. *Netting Your Ancestors: Genealogical Research on the Internet* (Baltimore, 1999)

KINEALY, C. *Tracing Your Irish Roots* (Belfast, 1991)

KINEALY C. and PARKHILL, T. (eds) *The Famine in Ulster* (Belfast, 1997)

LUCEY, M. 'Rateable Valuation in Ireland', in *Administration*, Spring 1964, vol. 12, no. 1

MacATASNEY, G. *The Famine in Lurgan and Portadown* (Dublin, 1997)

MacCONGHAIL, M. and GORRY, P. *Tracing Your Irish Ancestors* (Glasgow, 1997)

McCARTHY, T. *The Irish Roots Guide* (Dublin, 1991)

MacCUARTA, B. (ed) *Ulster 1641: Aspects of the Rising* (Belfast, 1993)

MacLYSAGHT, E. *Irish Families: Their Names, Arms and Origins* (Dublin, 1957)

MacLYSAGHT, E. 'Seventeenth Century Hearth Money Rolls', in *Analecta Hibernica*, no. 24

MAXWELL, I. *Tracing Your Ancestors In Northern Ireland* (Edinburgh, 1997)

MAXWELL, I. *Researching Armagh Ancestors* (Belfast, 2000)

MAXWELL, I. *Researching Down Ancestors* (UHF, 2004)

NEILL, K. *How to Trace Family History in Northern Ireland* (Belfast, 1986)

NOLAN, W. *Tracing the Past* (Dublin, 1982)

NOLAN, W. (ed) *The Shaping of Ireland: The Geographical Perspective* (Dublin, 1986)

O'NEILL, R.K. *Ulster Libraries: A Visitor's Guide* (Belfast, 1987)

O'SULLIVAN, H. 'The Magennis Lordship of Iveagh in the Early Modern Period, 1534 to 1691', in *Down: History and Society* (Dublin, 1997)

OUIMETTE, D.S. *Finding Your Irish Ancestors: A Beginner's Guide* (Ancestry, 2005)

PHAIR, P.B. 'Guide to the Registry of Deeds', in *Hibernica Analecta,* no. 3.

PROUDFOOT, L. (ed) *Down: History and Society* (Dublin, 1997)

QUINN, S.E. *Trace Your Irish Ancestors* (Wicklow, 1989)

RADFORD, D.A. and BETIT, K.J. *A Genealogist's Guide to Discovering Your Irish Ancestors* (Betterway Books, Ohio, 2001)

RAYMOND, S. *Irish Family History on the Web,* 2nd edn (Federation of Family History Societies, 2004)

ROBINSON, P. *The Plantation of Ulster* (Belfast, 1994)

RYAN, J.G. *Irish Records: Sources for Family and Local History* (Salt Lake City, 1988)

RYAN, J.G. *Irish Church Records* (Dublin, 1992)

RYAN J.G. *Sources for Irish Family History* (Dublin, 2001)

Index